THE ULTIMATE

By

Glendon Cameron

You can do far more than you think you can……..

I'm dedicating this book to my good friend FR; she introduced me to the world of garage sales. If it was not for her, more than likely I never would have ever become a part of the storage auction business. For that and more, I am truly grateful!

Copyright © Sept 2010 by Glendon Cameron

All rights reserved. No part of this book my be reproduced or transmitted in any form or by any means, electronic or mechanical including photocopying, recording or by any information storage and retrieval system, without written permission in writing from the Publisher.

Conundrum Publishing Company

Table of Contents

What Motivated Me To Write This Book?   7

A Nation of Clutter!   13

There is No Place like the Beginning!   18

Trash or Treasure It Really Doesn't Matter!   30

How Much Can I Get for This S***?   37

Show Me The MONEY!!!   44

The Longest Day (Best Garage Sale Days)   50

An Open Mouth Gets Fed- Spread The Word Baby!   57

Setting Up Your Sale   69

Garage Sale Signs (Home Made Are Best)   75

Your Day Of Reckoning!   93

For Storage Auction Addicts this is for You!   100

What motivated me to write this book?

I decided to write this book for people that want to learn how to have to garage sales based on storage auction inventories. **More about that in the last chapter**, the only difference between the person that has just a few garage sales and a storage auction buyer is the volume of inventory and sale management channels.

This book is also great for folks that just want to clear some stuff out of their homes and make extra money. When you have the possibility of getting different items every week and the opportunity to make money all in the same vein it is a beautiful thing! A garage sale is an awesome way to raise money quickly! **Storage unit auctions and garage sales go hand in hand**. Both pursuits attract the same type of people. Those that relish the thrill of the hunt, and just the thrill of finding a treasure! Something unique, something different, something useful and of course the biggest reason getting good stuff at a great price!

With storage auctions providing the inventories for your garage sales you can give your customers all of that and more! With my many years in the resale business, I have come to learn that people really like junk. Seriously, one man's trash is another man's treasure I know you have heard it over and over again, in the case of a garage sale sourced by storage auction finds there literally could be treasure in the junk! I have allowed certain items to sneak into the garage sale. Perhaps a gold chain or a diamond necklace, people love to find such things at a garage sale!

Making money on the side is one of the hottest topics in American culture right now. The economy sucks! Times are hard and people are doing everything that they can to survive. This is a great way for you to make extra money every year, sometimes monthly depending on where you live. The average person with a two car garage or 3 to 4 bedroom home can probably make an extra **$2000 to $5000** dollars a year part time with garage sales. Some people can make this per month!

If you're reading this book, it's clear that you want to make more than a few dollars and cents at your garage sale. More than $200 and you can do it with probably the stuff that's just lying around your house that you do not even need. If you have been reading my blog *"What Not To Leave In A Storage Unit"* you know I give it to you straight. This is not about easy money; it is going to take some effort planning and time to have a successful garage sale.

I made **$1350** on my first garage sale, it took time, and it was a lot of hard work. By following the guidelines I set forth in this book you will be able to generate that type of money or even more at your garage sale.

Most people do not t believe that you can make a lot of money at a garage sale. This is a good thing and this is a bad thing. Great news for you if you're shopping at a garage sale! Not so good for you, if you're holding the garage sale. One of the things you must do is dispel that misconception is to put on a hell of a garage sale, this book will show you how!

Over the years I have learned that you can make a great deal of money at a garage sale. **The key is preparation, marketing, enthusiasm and a smile.** Have you ever stopped by a garage sale and the people there having the sale did not even have the courtesy to say hello to you? Unless they had some really good stuff more likely you did not buy. The energy you put into a garage sale will yield the same type of dollars out of a garage sale.

Simply put, you get out of it what you put in it. The proper mindset is very critical in having a profitable garage sale. Many people have garage sales just to get rid of stuff, there's nothing wrong with that all. My thoughts on this are , if you are going to spend the time and energy in having a garage sale shouldn't you make as much money as possible?

The knowledge that you will gain from this book regardless of the type sale that you have **(garage sale, fund raising sale, estate sale, yard sale, bake off sale, church fund rasier)** will help you bring in more money than you normally would have made by not reading the book.

What I am going to give you in this book is really just common sense; it's not hard to do. By following the guidelines set forth in this book you can have a great sale! In taking the time to prepare for an organized, clean, well marketed and friendly garage sale, you may surprise your self with how much money you can make.

You may find this bit of information about me very funny. I was never ever, the type to go to a garage sale! I thought it was the refuge for people to put their funky, stinky and messy stuff out and hope some fool would buy it! I was the type of person that would drive by and never stop. Really thumb my nose up at folks having sales. Kind of uppity when I think about it now, most garage sales I saw looked like hell with chaos thrown in for good measure.

I'll be really honest, I was one of those snooty people that would never wear secondhand clothing or utilize secondhand merchandise. It is really funny now that in my **YouTube** videos I brag about the items that I have on are out of storage units! For years I never went to the mall to buy clothing or shoes. I got all of my clothing out of storage units for seven years straight. All of the clothes for my girlfriend my friends and my kids came out of storage units.

The biggest problem you going to have in hosting many garage sale are with your local zoning laws. <u>In some places you can have a garage sale every day of the week and no one cares.</u> In other places they will report you even when you're have authorization and permits!

There are really some snooty people in the world, just beware! So, before you make a huge investment in having lots of garage sales at your primary residence. Be very clear about what you are getting your self into. When I first started with the storage auction business, it all began with a garage sale. Who knew eight years later that I would be writing this book? Life is funny like that sometimes.

What I've seen other garage sales… yes I am a hater!

Oh let me tell you the troubles I have seen… damn I'm about to start with an old Negro spiritual! Some of those garage sales in fact did need salvation! You do not want to be that person, having a jacked up garage sales! Nothing is priced, things are in the state of disarray and the whole scene is very uninviting. **This is a major turn off!**

Not the fact that I never had one that went bad, all of the ones I had the misfortune to drive by were bad or unorganized. **After having that first and very successful garage sale I was hooked!** I got myself into trouble, after discovering a rich vein of inventory that one can gain from storage auctions. I was having garage sales every other weekend!

My neighbors were pissed. I think I know which one did it, yes that's right the so and so's turned me in to the man! I think it was the airline pilot; he really did not like the fact that we were having so many sales. He even came over a few times to be nosy; after he stopped coming over we got the notice in the mail. It was a cease and desist order. Essentially a warning and if we had in any more garage sales outside the parameters of the law that was set forth the first fine was **$200! I started to ignore it, we were making so much money I thought hey just chalk it up to a cost of business, and after further contemplation I stopped having so many garage sales.**

And if we were caught again the fines would increase! Thus, my journey begin into the flea market space, however that is another book. What I want you to think about is making your garage sale a happy event. Do not look upon it as some unwanted chore. This will decrease your chances for success tremendously. Mindset can be everything!

Look at it this way, a garage sale is a great opportunity to clean up your house gets rid of things you no longer want or can use and make some money! Everyone loves a deal! This is truly a one hand that washes the other scenario.

Viewed through that prism it is a horse of another color and the color is green all up in your pocket! Now let's discuss terminology. Some people call their sales a **garage sale**. Others will call their sale a **yard sale**. There's really no difference between the two. With one exception if you call your sale an **estate sale people will come to your sale with the expectation that you're selling everything!**

They will want go through your house all of the rooms and even the basement. With this information in mind just keep what you call your sale very simple. Call it a garage sale or yard sale or basement sale but never an estate sale unless you plan on selling everything in your house. More importantly than the name that you call your sale, is the set of rules I'm giving to you in this book that will make your sale successful.

A Nation of Clutter

Every year just before spring, you start to see the signs of the season changing. Usually those signs are in bold letters on bright cardboard paper. Spring cleaning produces spring garage and yard sales in spades. In locations where the temperatures are pretty consistent, this is a weekly event. In my neighborhood I counted 35 garage sales during one weekend. Where is all of this stuff coming from?

We live in a society of rampant consumers, spurred on by a social philosophy that the more that we have the happier we should be. This is one of the biggest lies on the planet! The end result of this mentality is the proliferation of garage, yard, basement and estate sales in North America on any given weekend.

Once I got in the resale business, I started to pay attention to garage sales and estate sales. My findings were very surprising! When I had the time I want to stop at every sale that I noticed there were a lot of great items at those sales. Sometimes **I would buy stuff from a garage sale and take it back to my store and sell 3, 4, 5 or 6 times as much!**

You'll see brand new stuff at garage sales, clothes, shoes and other items with the tags still affixed. **In my mind, ran this thought, did they really need this stuff to begin with?** Hey, it happens every day that someone buys something they really do not need. With this firm fixation of rabid consumerism there's going to be great garage sales for decades to come!

The United States of America is a nation of pack rats. There is this notion that if we bought it, it must be good or worth holding onto, even if holding on to that item is hurting us. When I would buy storage units, it always amazed me, how many brand new items that I got out of the storage units. In all of my years of buying the property of other people at auction, in roughly 60% of the units I bought, there were a few new items to many new items.

Sometimes the storage unit would be full of brand new items. I was over in the east part of town, Decatur Georgia. The auction crowd was slim, and they had 10 units up for sale. The first two units going up for auction belonged to a couple building a new house. Everything in both units was brand new! Brand new appliances, to completely new wardrobes for him and her were in those units!

When I got those two units, it hit me that we were a nation of pack rats. These good folks really did not need this stuff. Many times you get the back story from the storage auction manager, this couple ran into financial problems and took their money and built a smaller house.

Yes, you read me correctly; they just let all of this stuff go because they did not need it! There is this tendency in our society to hold on to things. **Earlier this year, there was an article online about the lady paying $800 a month to store items from her recently foreclosed house** She was unemployed. It never occurred to her to sell the stuff she was storing. Her story ends very sadly, she paid well over $19,000 to store stuff that may have been worth $12,000 and she ended up losing both units in an auction!

She would have come out so much better liquidating both of the storage units and moving on with her life. But she did not; her story is very common the only difference is the size of what is being held on to for dear life. **Are you holding onto things in your life that have absolutely no purpose to you at the present moment?** Maybe, just maybe it is time to let that stuff go.

I am not talking about your wedding pictures, or your first great report card, nope I am not talking about any of that stuff. W hat I am talking about are the eight sets of golf clubs in your house. Or the 250 pair shoes in your closet, some dating back to your high school years. Why are you holding on to this stuff? It doesn't fit and no one is using it!

Okay, that is it of my social commentary about our nation of clutter. Let's get on with the funky stuff, you are reading this book for a reason. You want to host a profitable garage sale. It will be easier than you think, just take a few moments to read this book and come up with your game plan before you do anything! I am really big into setting goals.

 As you go through the book, I left space for you to make notes. I want you to make notes, when you are not thinking about something that is when it enters into your mind! After reading this book, I want you to get a notebook and right on the cover inscribe "**MY GARAGE SALE JOURNEY**" this will be a way to keep your self organized, or it you are a computer person create a word document with the same title. **Confucius said "short pencil is better than long memory" it is very true!** By been organized and prepared you will have one heck of a garage sale.

Thing to Do!

Write down your goals and create an action plan. There will be more about how to do this, later on in the book. Written goals have a tendency to achieve their selves. Yes, I know this is a little weird, but I've come across goals written in old notebooks years ago that I never looked at again that I have accomplished. There something special about taking what is in your mind and placing it on paper or the computer screen that gives it life and energy to make it come to fruition.

You may also find a strange byproduct to this whole process, in going around your house and getting rid of stuff or I should say making decisions to get rid of stuff. You'll start to feel lighter and a little freer. I have been through this process several times. Today I no longer hold on to things that do not serve me well, you will find this incredibly liberating when you get to this point in your life. It is amazing what you can find at a garage sale even your own!

Don 't be scared be prepared!

Notes

Notes!

There is No Place like the Beginning

Are you ready to rumble? Good! Let's get started!

The first place that you're going to start is with the stuff. What is stuff you may ask? It is anything in your house that you do not need or want, literally anything! From the roota to the toota as I like to say!

Yes those old jeans in the corner. That lamp that your grandmother gave to you, that you have in a closet, which is only taken out when she comes over for Christmas. I want you to open up your mind. Many of the things, that you think are total trash, someone will buy very cheaply.

I mean anything! The gambit ranges from half empty perfume bottles to the markers that your kids no longer use. It's all in the packaging and marketing. You will be very surprised at the things that are in your home that you forgot about. Assessing the items in your home that you no longer want or use is the key to making money.

Those old eight track tapes, the chicken suit that your son wore on his part time job. To you this is junk to others it is treasure. You are going to go through every drawer, closet, under the bed, under the sofa, all of the cabinets in your kitchen and of course the attic, garage and basement.

Step one -sit down in your easy chair have a drink and decide which room you going to do first. There is a systematic method to gathering up your stuff. In your everyday life you tend to hide or disregard things that you'll don't want because you do not want to deal with that stuff. Like that closet in the hallway, that every time you open the door stuff falls out.

We as Americans have a love affair with our clutter, we love to hate it and we love to not deal with it. **In the average American home, there's probably enough stuff for a $1000 to $1500 garage sale or even more!** There are many items that you have all over the place, right now in your house taking up space and driving you crazy.

This book is going to be two parts, the first section is about getting your home ready for the stuff you already have! It makes no sense at all, to have a garage sale with storage auction stuff before you clean up the stuff you all ready have in your home. The second part will be for the storage auction enthusiast, you will have some special requirements the average garage seller will never think about!

Please bear with me, before you put the roof on any house you must have a solid foundation are you just going to have a mess on your hands.

I want you to go through your house like a Ninja! This is the time to channel you're inner accountant. You are no longer you; you're a lean, mean sorting machine. You will go through each and every room in your house with a fine tooth comb. It does not matter which room that you start in, the important thing is to get started.

While you're in that easy chair sipping on your mojito, create a set of goals for yourself. The number one goal is to identify all unwanted items in every room. I want to give you some criteria to help you make these decisions.

The Six Commandments

1. If you have not worn an article of clothing in the last two years it's got to go!

2. If you have not used this item in the last six months and is not a seasonal item it's got to go!

3. If it no longer fits and I do not care how cute it is it's got to go!

4. If your kids have toys that they no longer play with (include them in on this decision making process) they have got to go!

5. If you cannot get in your garage and all of the items in the garage serve no purpose what so ever, all have to go!

6. If it is falling out of the closet, it has got to go!

If the mojito is gone, time to get cracking! Now that you're all mellow and relaxed grab a sheet of paper. This is where you are going to create your master plan. I am very big on writing everything down, this helps keep me organized and the project on track. This also includes entering it into your Iphone or Blackberry. The point is to have your thoughts, goals and process fully formulated before you start doing anything. For those of you that do not drink get yourself some fruit punch! Make this an object of fun, it can be if you just stay in the moment, do one thing at a time versus creating a massive project in your mind before you even begin!

What Really Needs to Go! (this is a notes page, in disguise!)

Action Plan Example.

> Dear Self,
>
> Today's date is March 3 2010 I am having my Garage Sale on July 10 2010Each week I will go through a section of my home identify items for the garage sale. I will devote not less than two hours a week to get this accomplished.
>
> All designated garage sale items will be boxed and placed in my garage until the time of the sale.
>
> 1 my bedroom
>
> 2 the kids bedroom
>
> 3 guest room
>
> 4 all second floor closets
>
> 5 kitchen
>
> 6 dining room
>
> 7 family room
>
> 8 living room
>
> 9 office
>
> 10 all first floor closet
>
> 11 basement
>
> 12 garage

I believe the most important thing about prepping for a garage sale is the organization. This is the stage that will determine if you're going to have the average garage sale or a killer garage sale! By using the example of my action plan on the page before you will save yourself a lot of time and stress.

The biggest part of a garage sale is deciding what you are going to sell or throw away. This can be really stressful for some people! Do not over think it! Some items will need to be thrown away. I call this the purge stage. These items are beyond repair, or there is something really wrong with these items. Because space, for some of you reading this book is going to be a premium. There will be some choices to be made about what is going to the garage sale or not. Usually these items that you meant to throw away, you just haven't gotten around to it as of yet. There shouldn't be too much of this stuff, however, every one is different.

Do you have your have your ninja suit on? Okay, you really do not need a ninja suit. Just wear something comfortable. The process of going through your home and gathering all of these items for your garage sale is going to take a long time. Take that frown off you face, you knew this was coming!

That is why we are going to break up the elephant into little pieces. By this, I mean you're going to have a plan of calculated attack. You have a life, job and family one of the goals of this book is to make this process as painless as possible. By identifying what needs to go and creating goals to guide you in achieving these ends, you will get it done and not lose your sanity. **It is all about the organization baby!**

The very first thing that you want to do is set the date for a garage sale. Today is May 1st and you want to have a garage sale 90 days from now. That is almost 12 weekends to get this done and not interfere with your normal life. What we are going to do is a little bit of prep at a time. This is just a loose time frame you can have it sooner or later it all depends on you. **By starting now and doing a little bit at a time, you can make a monumental task such as a large garage sale a piece of cake!**

The gist of this plan is to do one section, of one room at a time. If you are a all or nothing type of person, you can knock out a room at a time. There is no right or wrong way to do this, the guidance given here is to help the time challenged person accomplish the goal of getting ready for their garage sale.

Let's take the kitchen, you have 30 free minutes. Take this time to go through all of the drawers, under the kitchen sink and all of the cabinets. Have a box or bag handy, place all of the items you want to sell in the box and mark it garage sale.
 You've just cleaned out a section of your house and it took 30 minutes, maybe less, you are one step closer to having your garage sale. This is why it pays to have a note book, you can log your process, cross off sections in your home, that you complete, the feeling of accomplishment will make you feel better! Since you are going to be all over your home, the notebook also makes it easy to keep up with which rooms your have competed.

This is the process that you're going to utilize to prep for your garage sale. Take your bedroom, for example, usually unless you're very fastidious there something of value under the bed. In your closet, not just the obvious but stuff in the back, stuffed under stuff! You bought this stuff it had value to you at one point, someone else will see the value in it also.

Essentially anything can be sold at a garage sale. **My school of thought, if it sold once, it will sell again.** I have actually seen stuff at garage sales with Goodwill tags on them! (well they write the price in crayon on their items) **Now that is what you call recycling!**

Even if the item is broken, such as a bicycle or maybe even an appliance if you sell it cheap enough someone will buy it. If you just want to get rid of it, put a **FREE** sign on it. Do not discount anything in your mind. **When in doubt put it out!** You will be surprised at what sells that your garage sale. People from all walks of life, have different needs and wants. I say this so you will not censor yourself. Don't say nobody would want this or is too old to sell. Everything except decrepit old stinky things will sell.

Here's a hint; anything that is name brand that is in serviceable condition can be sold, it is really a matter of price. Enclosed are a few things that you probably have never even thought about selling. Say for example that laundry detergent that you bought used a little bit of it and decided that you did not like it anymore. Someone will buy that stuff from you! Your old coworker gave you an extra laptop bag with the company name on it, yes it will sell! I have even sold corporate branded coffee cups at a garage sale and the guy came back for more, I guess he really enjoyed his coffee! Remember you are in Ninja mode! Take yourself out of the picture and think like some one that is looking for a deal!

This is totally up to you, but you can price the items as you source the items. **A GOOD FREAKIN IDEA** Before you put it in the box or that bag for the garage sale you can affix a price on it. As you are placing items in the bag or the box, price each item, this will save you a ton of time! This way you're killing two birds with one stone, yes I am fond of clichés! I find having marker, labels and a stapler with me as I identified garage sale items makes the job of pricing go so much faster. If you wait until a few days before your sale, top price the items, you will be doing double work, **NOT A GOOD LOOK** we are efficient Ninjas!

Being a process guy I like to break up projects in little bitty pieces. As you go through the steps of prepping for this garage sale you will start to feel a sense of accomplishment on each leg of the journey that is done. There is just something very satisfying about looking at your action plan and seeing items being marked off one by one.

Most Items At your Sale will Be under $20.00

As you are gathering items for your garage sale, and writing the price on the item, you will notice most items and to be well under $20.00. Don't even worry about that, you will make your money on volume. I have had garage sales were nothing was over $15.00 and still did over $1000 on the sale. Believe me when you sell hundreds of items it adds up quickly!

If over the course of your to three day garage sale, you sold 250 different items with an average selling price of $3.75 look at the end result! **250 x 3.75= $937.50**

Items That Sell At Garage Sales (a small list)

Fake fruit
Bookshelves these are highly desired and fast sellers!
Space heaters
Christmas decorations
Safes
Auto parts
Musical instruments
Old posters
Fireplace tools
Folding tables
Stack tables sets
Appliances
Old magazines
Hand towels and bath towels
Old clothing
Fancy shower curtains
Stuffed animals
Unwanted wedding gifts
Old backpacks
Camping equipment
Kitchen container sets
Fancy salt and pepper sets
Picture frames and photo labs
Used crayons and art supplies
Stereo equipment
Hotel soap and shampoo-put it in a bag and sell it as a set.
Over the counter drugs –make sure that they're not expired!
Computers
Old records
Cassette tapes
Books

Soap
Art
Shoes
Clothing
Jewelry
Throw pillows
Socks
Underwear-believe it or not people will buy used underwear!
Linen
Lawnmowers
Tools
China
Pots and pans
Carpet
Fitness equipment-weather works or not
T V's
Anything old or vintage
Furniture
Accent I teams
Used candles
Incense
Buttons
Sewing machines
Nails and screws
Used paint interior or exterior
Leftover hardwood floor remnants
Car tools
Power tools
Carpet
Flooring
Towels
Dog cages
Stuffed animals

Old doorknobs
Avon
Mary Kay
Shingles
Sheet rock
Brakes
Stone
Car parts
Wood
Cheap toys
Knick knacks
Pressure washer
Rims

Everything on this list is something that I have sold at a garage sale. When I say people will buy anything at a garage sale I am not kidding!

Trash or Treasure It Really Doesn't Matter!

Right now your mind is just buzzing with information and new ideas! How do I know what is a good item to sell? Should I just throw it in the trash? This is a very good question and I have the answer for you. It really doesn't matter, what you think is trash! **(Other than the obvious)** say you have some pots missing the lids, they will sell! Remember it is about the price of the thing you are selling, clearly things missing components should be priced by the cheap pen.

Think about it, normal and everyday items, that is what sells at garage sales. You really don't have to have super nice stuff. **I am 100% serious**! I sold bricks at one garage sale! Yes, a pallet of bricks, I got out of a storage unit, a contractor drove by and inquired about the bricks, they were not even part of the sale! I had then in my driveway until I could move them. I told him a $350.00; he thrust the money in my hand and started loading them! A new pallet of bricks can be anywhere from $600-$1200.00! Yes, he got a deal! As I said before, if you are in doubt, put it out!

What you do have to sell, should be clean, functional and well presented, a great set up can do wonders for normal stuff! This is what will make your garage sale a winner!

The exceptions, Ha Ha Ha!

You knew this was coming; just place items that kind of sort of, still work, on a separate table. Mark these items very cheaply between $1.00 and $10.00 or free even, depending upon the item. Your goal is to get these items out of your house, so any offer is a good offer for something that you are probably more than likely will throw away at some point! Just check out my list of items that sell at garage sales, nothing is off the table. I do mean nothing!

Broken plasma or LCD T V's still have value, someone will buy them just for the parts. Certain electronic items such as broken laptops, damaged iPods, old cell phones, radios, stereo receivers, small household appliances and old tools hold value to people that like to tinker or actually need that part. **When in doubt put it out!** If it doesn't sell just toss it. The goal for these debatable items is to get it out of your house! My advice on this stuff is if it does not sell the first time, toss it! Better items that do not sell the first time you will keep, until your next sale.

Let us talk about grandmother's China from old world Germany. Here is a very harsh and cold truth; **most of you are not going to have priceless antiques in your home**. You may have what is really a vintage piece that does have value. Not everyone is going on the *Antique Road Show.* One exception to this is, is the storage auction buyer, you have a very good chance of coming across items of that persuasion! If will be up to you to sell it at the garage sale or an antique auction, once you do your research on the item you will have your answer. Generally if the item is not in excellent, great or good condition it is not worth taking to auction, however, **always conduct your due diligence on the piece! Better to know, than to assume!**

For people that have vintage or antique types of items, just set those pieces aside and consult someone. If you have a local auction house, just e-mail them a few pictures. Take note of this fact, if they want your stuff or not should tell you a lot! **You must realize that auctions are also very risky.** It could be a very valuable item, it depends on who's at the auction and how bad that they want it. If the item is marginal, meaning is not likely to bring a lot of money, is up to you to decide is it worth selling are holding onto.

For those that have a house full of true antiques and vintage items. You're better off having an estate sale or hiring an auction house. You will make more money with an estate sale, unless you have high grade antiques with providences intact, then the auction house is the best way to go. Some auction houses or auctioneers will bring the auction to you, if you have enough items for the auction house to present to its regular bidders. I ran the contents of five units through an auction house and made $20,000.00 in four hours! We really did $25,000 the auction house got 20% of the sale.

One of the problems with having a sale is many people do not know how to let go of things. **When you were in your easy chair with your mojito did you really prepare yourself to let go of these items? For some this will be the hardest part! I cannot stress this enough, let go man or wo-man!**

Many people have sentimental attachment to a lot of stuff. My question to you, how are you a incorporate the sentimental stuff into your everyday life? I've made a lot of deliveries and I have been in a lot of homes.

There are great many people who are using grandmother's hutch, table set, bedroom set, flatware and other useful items. This is a great way to show your respect and gain use out of the piece versus allowing it to gain dust in the basement. If you're the type of person that is paying a ton of money storing this stuff, it is in boxes in your basement and you have not looked this stuff in years. **Perhaps, today is the day to let that stuff go!**

My philosophy is going to be different from most. I do not believe in holding onto stuff just to hold onto it. This is how your house becomes a haven of overflowing with crap! If you are going to keep it use it! That should be your rule of thumb. I know in your head, you'd think in this guy is crazy.

I built a business based on people having too much crap! Whenever, I bought a storage unit, nine times out of ten, those same people had similar items wherever they were. Simply put, they did not need to stuff that was in storage. **It is a little ridiculous, when you think about it, paying money to store stuff you do not need**!

Most people that do need the stuff in storage, usually it is kept in storage only for a short term, a few weeks or a few months and is out of the storage unit back into their home or new home. If you have items in storage for years and years you may want to talk to yourself over a cup of coffee!

Rule of Thumb For Keeping Stuff in Storage Versus Selling it!

Cost and true need should drive your decision, not I want it just in case I need it. The average storage space costs $75.00 per month that is $900.00 dollars a year! If the stuff you are storing is only worth a thousand dollars you just threw tons of money away in a year. Say you store your stuff for two years; your personal balance sheet is bleeding red! **That is almost $2000.00 spent to hold to stuff worth a thousand dollars, what is wrong with this math?**

The $75.00 space is a mid size space, the losses grow larger with a bigger storage space! The space that had the fire truck in it was $299.00 per month seven years ago! **That is $3600.00 a year in storage costs!** I included this section, because, many of you reading this book have stuff in storage. The cost of the storage unit is on auto pay, you do not even think about it, yet those are real dollars going to waste every month! If you are not even thinking about the items in storage, you do not miss any of it, there is a very good reason, **you don't need it!**

Now we're ready to get busy. You are ready to rock and roll, your mind is clear you've got your parameters set. Yes, it is time to begin to clean up your life as well as your house. This is deeper than just clutter in your home. **Trust me, when you relieve yourself of all of these items that are just holding you down, you will feel so much better!**

Just getting started will give you an emotional boost, if you're taking action and solving a dilemma in your life, that is a good thing too! I go much deeper than most about the psychology of pack rats. Being in a resale business for many years, you'll know the look of a pack rat. Many will tell you that there a pack rat, I really don't need this. I've heard to so many times, following a sale,**" I really should not be buying this"** I should have my own garage sale! They are not kidding; we live in a culture that teaches us buying stuff makes us happy. As I stated before, nothing could be further from the truth.

Check List!

∴ Write up your action plan

∴ Designate a area to stockpile your garage sale inventory

∴ Do one section of one room at a time until you are finished with that room!

∴ Price items as you gather them, saves time! Less work!

∴ Ascertain if you have any true antiques and do your legwork on the best channels to sell those items.

∴ Get rid of the trash! Purge baby purge!

Notes!

How much can I get for this S*&^! ?

This is a $64,000 question, how much money can I make at a garage sale?

In my personal experience you can make a lot of money at a garage sale. This is truly a case of you will get what you ask for. Pricing the items that you're gathering for a garage sale is not rocket science. It is a matter of having an ideal of what the fair market price of a used item is. Many people just give their stuff away because they want it out of the house. In one vein they are successful, their goal is to get the stuff out of their house and they do. There is no real regard to actually making substantial money at the garage sale and thus, they do not.

Don't sell yourself short; more likely you paid a lot of money for some of the stuff that is lying around your house. For a fair price someone else will give you more than pennies for those same items that you are not using. If you're truly convinced of the worth of an item others will follow suit. It is a case of, if you think it, so will they.

The biggest reason that you're doing this **is to make money.** That is your single reason for buying this book, going through your home, and setting up for your garage sale. Keep that single goal in mind at all times! Staying focused will help you as you prep for your garage sale.

Pricing is like making love; everyone knows how to do it but everyone doesn't do it well!

I wish I could give you a template this with all of prices on it. But I can't. The reason is you know what is in your home better than I would. Another factor is size, condition, time of year and your location. People in nicer neighborhoods can get more money. I have seen this fact, with my own eyes to many times to count. I have been to numerous garage sales and I have seen people fork over almost 80% of the retail price in a ritzy neighborhood. I have also seen people in those same ritzy neighborhoods practically give stuff away to get rid of it. It is truly a mixed bag garage sale shopping in a well to do neighborhood!

I was at a garage sale once, where the woman that was hosting the sale, asked me to hook up her stereo equipment. It was an old Kenwood rack system, very simple to hook up. It had been in her basement for years! Once I got it going the sound was amazing! She sold it within minutes! While I was setting up her audio equipment I noticed how she would interact with the other buyers at the garage sale. She was very polite and very firm. Always smiling and it worked!

This lady knew the value of her items and stuck to her guns on some items and took whatever on other things in the sale, it was clear she had a knack for this type of thing. You will find out in a moment, why she was so good at selling. She had many articles of name brand clothing and several pieces of high in furniture. Mixed in with those very nice quality items, were many run of the mill everyday type stuff. As I watched her sell stuff, I thought to myself I've seen better stuff go for less, her presentation was awesome! Before I left, I asked her how often she had sales, she said this was her first one but she owned a retail store for three decades and if there was one thing she knew how to do, it was sell! It showed, she was cleaning up loot wise!

One of the reasons that a lot of people do not make huge money at a garage sale is that they under cut their prices. Do not be scared to price your items for what you really think their worth. An example would be a Ralph Lauren or POLO shirt, brand new these are very expensive pieces of clothing. I would not hesitate to pay $5.00 to almost $20.00 for a POLO shirt in great condition. In the store I would pay $50.00 or more for this same shirt. It's the way that you look at it that shows you, if it is a deal or not.

I know that we we're in a recession and times are tough for many people. This does not mean everything has to be at rock bottom prices, not even at a garage sale!

One thing that I have noticed about the people in the United States of America is we like to spend money!

In doing this we also love a deal, a garage sale will accomplish both ends. Do not let the hard times lull you into thinking you have to sell everything dirt cheap to make money at your garage sale. Some things, yes, they need to be dirt cheap, because in the grand scheme of things that is what they are really worth.

To help demystify the science of pricing I want to give you a few pointers. Taking note of condition, how common this item is, **(the more common it is the cheaper it should be)** and what the market will bear. **Example-**I had a go kart that I got out of a storage unit I bought at auction. The room cost me $120, the price online of the go kart was selling for $600-795.00 (online pricing can be screwy at times). Just looking at the go kart you could not tell it was not new. I put the go kart front and center of the garage sale was a price of $650 and put some tire dressing on the wheels, made it look hot!

The first guy who saw the go kart offered me $200.00 right there on the spot, which I pleasantly declined. If you are offered a price of less than half of what you are asking these folks are seeking a killer deal, the deal is the most important aspect of the transaction, more important than the item! Rarely will you come to terms with these people, it best to put your energy into other customers. You, don't have to be mean about it, but disengage yourself as quickly as possible from these people. They will take up a lot of time and not buy anything!

 The third person they came up and inquired about it bought it from me for $580. (I would have taken $500.00) Her son wanted that very same go kart for his birthday. She saw they were selling for $650 to $790 plus tax and shipping if she bought it online. She had her eye on it for months!

She was what I called an educated buyer; she knew it was a deal as soon as she saw it. Someone that just wanted go kart and had not done any research would have thought an opening price of $650 was insane at a garage sale! She saved a lot and did not have to pay tax or shipping!

Notes-online pricing is s significantly less that offline pricing just know if you do your research online items are going to be more in the store. I understand this 2010 but there are many people who do not comparison shop!

Another example-I bought a unit, this guy was a **Tony Robbins fanatic!** He had every book, cd, ideal tape and even some videos of Tony Robbins. There must've been 300 pieces of Tony Robbins material. I priced everything between $1.00 and $5.00. Lucky for me, another Tony Robbins fanatic showed up at my garage sale!

He asked me what I wanted for everything. The unit cost me $10.00. I paused for a few seconds and said "well I was asking between $1.00 and $5.00 per item, there are over 300 items that would just be $300 on everything if I sold each piece for a dollar. Since you want everything and you're helping me out what about $200 for everything? He looked around for a second and counter offered $180 which I took before he could change this mind!

At a garage sale you will have to be flexible, that is part of the garage sale culture, but you do not have to give the house away! I frequently, took offers that were 20% -25% below my asking price, sometimes even more depending on the day of the sale and what I had in the items, which was usually not a much. Some items I knew I could get my asking price, because of my marketplace research and I would not budge much on the price, at the most a 10% price reduction on items in that category.

When I entered the storage auction business, there was not a lot of information online or in the library for that matter. Things are very different today, for most items you will have three very handy resources. **Google, eBay and Craigslist** these websites will show you what an item is worth and also what the market will bear. Using these online resources will help you cut out a lot of the guesswork on your items.

Money Tip- Factor in the shipping in your price, the customer does! This means you can raise your offline item price a little or a lot base on the item in question!

As you are doing your research and gathering items for your sale you may realize that you can make more money selling these items on eBay are Craigslist versus your garage sale. Before you start posting your stuff of willy nilly for sale online, keep in mind your goal is to make this much money as possible while being efficient.

If you decide to sell the items on Ebay our Craigslist wait until you get up everything in your house sourced, before listing the items on either site This will prevent you from putting up a piece one week, then posting an item online the next week thus creating more work for yourself. I believe in grouping activities to create greater efficiencies and ease of accomplishing any task.

The Exceptions

Every one is unique, with that perspective each house is going to have different levels of merchandise. I referenced earlier if you have really nice stuff they would be best to have an estate sale. **Only have an estate sale if you're selling everything!**

The psychology behind the estate sale is everything is going to be sold. That brings out more people and they bring more money, because they expect to see something really good and valuable. Setting expectations as part of your marketing plan is a crucial step. One of the best ways to meet and exceed expectations is to be the architect of those expectations. When you pause on that thought, it really is your show!

This is why I say; do not have an estate sale unless you're selling everything. People will come to your estate sale with the expectation everything's up for sale. It is your entire garage; many people will not even stop! They will keep driving because they have no faith in you and what you're selling.

Do not attempt to sell priceless items at your garage sale. You and your customers both will be very frustrated. You want more money than they want to give. There are looking for a steal of a deal. There are other venues to sell those items. Later on in this book I will give you some pointers on how to move those items.

If you have guns that you want to sell, seek out a gun show in your area or talk to your local gun dealer. Some places in the country you can legally sell, long guns or rifles with no problem. **(I would check the gun laws in your area first!)** Be very careful with weapons and other dangerous items. Do not sell anything that is a illegal this includes food at your garage sale. As you can see there's not much that you can't sell a garage sale. Just be careful and use common sense on what you sell at your sale and you will be good to go!

Show Me The Money!

Remember that phrase from *Jerry Maguire*? That is your new personal anthem. To meet expectations is one of the best ways to get people to show you the money. Another is to market to those people in the manner they appreciate. The big thing that people are looking for the garage sale is a deal or what is perceived to be a deal. Perception, can everything!

Notice I did not say the lowest price? A deal is subjective, what one person may think is fantastically expensive; another person WILL snatch it up because the deal is just too good to be true!

This is how you get people to show you the money. What you do in all aspects of your garage sale from the layout, to the items, to the signs on the street all our marketing your garage sale.

Pricing is also another key component to your marketing plan, be creative in your pricing. Items you would ask a dollar for make it two for a dollar; I did not price items using cents! It is a pain and it takes more time to collect change than dollars!

Add more stuff to the sale package of smaller stuff to get dollar vs. change. If you have 100 Match box cars, put them in bags, in groups of ten, priced at $5.00 dollars, instead of selling each car for 50¢ selling methods like this, make a huge difference in the mind of your customer! **They feel like they are getting more bang for their buck and you are selling more stuff faster for a higher price!**

Do not use the dollar signs or the cents symbol (if you used cents in your pricing plan) In our society we are programmed to be desensitized to marketing, because so many people are doing the same exact thing in the same exact manner. **After seeing this so many times we automatically tune it out.** How many times do you zone out when commercials come on TV?

It is the same thing for your sale; you must be different to be seen as different! By making these small adjustments with your pricing you stand out.

Another way to get people to show you the money is by giving them bread crumbs. Bread crumbs are those small very inexpensive items that you have at the entrance of your sale. Also put eye catching items in places that are easily seen. **Example-many people tried to sell furniture at a garage sale. What they do is leave the furniture inside of the garage in the event that it doesn't sell so they will not have to move it again.**

What they're really doing is ensuring that it doesn't sell! Many people do drive by garage selling, if there is nothing inviting outside they do not even stop. I know it is extra work, but is worth it!

Note- any furniture you have for sale, make sure it is completely set up! Yes, that means you would put the bed together! Items people feel that are incomplete they will not buy and many will not ask about it!

Put those big items outside the furniture, the appliances, the toolbox and anything else that is big bright and eye catching. What you're telling your perspective customers is you have nice stuff and they need to stop and come on in to see what you have! If you have a colorful flag or even one of those large blow up decorations use it at the entrance of your sale.

I routinely put out ***"Herman"*** an 8 foot tall blow up Halloween decoration. I had dude out in the middle of summer and so many people stopped because of it! Things like that get you noticed! I bet you have never seen something like that at a garage sale! If you had, you surely would have stopped! **Things like that are exciting!**

A another way to get people to show you the money is to make sure that all your items are properly priced and labeled.

This is very true in terms of clothing items. You want each article of clothing to be labeled, priced and on that label you will have the size of the item. Make sure none of the clothing is wrinkled. People will not buy something that's wrinkled, a little dirt is not a problem but wrinkles will kill your sale. **Never expected to hear that nugget of wisdom now did you? It can be a little dirty, being wrinkled will not cut it.**

On your clothing items, make sure that there are easily accessible. I went to a garage sale years ago; there was a huge pile of clothing on a tarp. I was there for about 40 minutes it was a huge garage sale and I noticed that hardly anyone went over there to look over the clothing in the pile.

As I was leaving the garage sale, I noted there were a lot of brand name items in that pile. I've offered the owner of

$20.00 for the whole lot of clothing on the tarp. Long story short, I made over $500.00 dollars of those clothes!

Most folks are not going to go through a pile of clothing. I knew this and I took those clothes home washed them and put them in my store. Same items, vastly different results, this illustrates the difference between having a properly organized garage sale and not having one. Your clothing items have to be labeled and priced and accessible to sell.

During your sale you're going to be one busy beaver. **(Have as much help at you sale as possible)** As people are buying stuff you want to refresh your tables and rearrange the clothing items. This accomplishes two things that puts your best foot and greets new visitors to your garage sale with fresh tables and great deals. You want your areas to be nice and neat. Poorly organized tables equates to poor sales. **Do not crowd the tables! People want room to operate and shop! It is distress to someone to move one items and knock another one on the floor!**

You want to have your nicer items on a rack. Be careful where you place the rack. If you are in a windy area or it is windy that day the racks will be blown down and scatter clothing all over the place. If wind is not a problem you still want to be careful with clothing.

I always keep items on the rack inside and other clothing items in boxes grouped together by size on the outside. This makes it easy for people to go through the clothing. **DO NOT CRAM AS MANY CLOTHES IN THE BOXES AS POSSIBLE!!!!! If people have to work they will not buy!**

When you have a lull go through each box and straighten out the clothing and put back the mixed up items, this will happen.

When you have a crowd, people compete with each other to get to certain items! It is somewhat funny to watch!

In this race things are moved out of order. I suggest going to the dollar store to buy your labels. In this case a bigger is better, the nicer the item that you, sale the nicer the label should be. This is also marketing! Don't worry it's not going to cost you a lot of money. You can get thousands of labels for under $5.00. Make sure that your printing is legible.

Going back to my people are not going to work at a garage sale mantra, you need to make this as easy as possible for would be buyers of your garage sale merchandise.

Make sure your item description is clear and concise. I would lump cheaper items together as packages versus having penny stuff. Example those paints and markers you bought your child and they lost interest within a day. Instead of trying to sell the pieces put all in a freezer bag and put $5.00 or $4.95 (if you are a change person) on it. I have moved a lot of inventory this way! Be creative, people love that in a garage sale!

When you are in the dollar store and they have those really cool, colored coded labels and you are about to buy them, don't! **Color coded labels are like crack to the dishonest and unethical**, there is no way you can remember all of those prices, so take care and so not use color coded labels! The additional work will pay off!

Clean and orderly Makes Money!

I want you to think about when you go into a regular store; if, as soon as you walk in the place it is uninviting, that really sets the tone for the rest of your time in the store. If it is bad enough, you may never go back! Unfortunately, we live in the society where first impressions are lasting impressions.

This matriculates down to the garage sale in your neighborhood. Knowing this, you want to put best foot forward. By having a good looking garage sale that is clean, neat and that says, come on in and buy something, is the way to get people to show you the money!

The Longest Day!

Are you excited yet?

Well, whoa Nellie! Before you get too deep in your garage sale preparation, you absolutely positively need to know the law of the land. In some places no one gives a hoot about your garage sale. You can have as many as you want, as frequently as you want. That is not the case, in most parts of the country. Each town, city and metropolitan area has a set of rules on the books about garage sales. **YOU NEED TO KNOW THESE RULES MY FRIEND!**

In the quest of becoming the garage sale king of my area I ran a foul of the law. I did not even know that I was doing anything wrong. It took four months for them to catch up with me. No one ever came out, just got a notice in the mail. **The fines can be substantial so please take note of this section.**

I have noticed a neighbor is having garage sales every weekend; this has gone on for the last 6 months! I do not know if this is a sign of the economy, but clearly she is getting away with it! I would never NARC on her, I admire her drive!

I mean I was cranking it out! When you do more than **$1000** a week in garage sale money it becomes a little addictive! Making that type of money from the comfort of home was pretty nice! However, the law is the law. If you have a homeowners association, please check with them also. More than likely it will not be a problem, but there are some to crazy homeowner associations out there in the last thing you want to do is piss them off.

This is one of the things you want to do while getting ready for your sale. An additional note, some places require that you have a permit or license to have your garage sale. Crazy, I know but to stay within the letter of the law you have to do it.

Believe it or not, the longest day of your garage sale will be the day before! That is the day that you make sure everything is just so. The best days for garage sales are from my experience will be **Thursday, Friday and Saturday**. Sunday's can be okay, but it's usually not that great.

I have had garage sales every day of the week. But it never fails to come down to those three days as the best days to have your garage sale. I always assumed this was because everyone had garage sales on that day and that brought the crowd out. What is strange, is how many people will stop at your sale on their way to work on a Friday, no other day of the week will people do this! Walking quickly, looking at their watches, it always cracked me up!

If you are a garage sale hound, you know the deal. How many times have your seen other garage sale folks at different sales? I know I was over in Dunwoody and I saw the same folks at 15 different garage sales!

You can have a 2-6 day sale or even a 7 day sale. If you have a lot of stuff the sale can go on for weeks, I have seen it! I only did the 6 day sale when I was moving, most often it is 2-3 days and I am done. My days were Thurs- Sat mostly. I did a few Sunday sales, like I said before the results were disappointing; I have made more money on a Monday sale!

When is the best time to have a garage sale? Whenever you want! Of course within in the time frames set forth by your local governing body. I found that the weekend sales work best for my schedule. Now there are some of you who will be able to do the Monday through Saturday schedule with no problem. Which means you will make more money!

A properly advertised three day sale can do very well. My record for a garage sale, was $1350 in one day! Please understand I was getting my merchandise out of storage auction unit. This gave me a tremendous variety of product that you will not see at most garage sales.

When I had sales utilizing the items from my home, the average was $400 to $500 per day on a three out on a three day sale that averages out to well over a $1000 and it all depends on what you have at the sale and how well it is marketed. Sometimes, I made far more! It would be significantly more, if I had furniture and nice electronics at my sale. These numbers are to show you what you can make with regular run of the mill stuff.

What is the best time to have a garage sale?

The earlier the better! Most garage sales stall around **3:00 PM -4:00 PM** . So to take full advantage of that time frame, I would start my sales around 7:00 AM during the warmer months. And I would start my sales around 10:00 AM doing the colder months. The reason for the late start when it gets colder is most people do not want to get out of bed on a cold morning if they have a choice! I know this from having of years and years of garage sales. Also, very few other people are having sales so this is a diehard garage sale shopper's dream to find a sale in the off-season.

Note- if you say open to 5:00PM there is usually another rush that can keep you there for a while! On the times I got caught, it usually was another hour! You can end your sale at any time. As long as people were there spending money I stayed open. On garage sale days, I schedule nothing else, you will be tired after!

I am in Georgia where it doesn't get that cold during the winter as a result I have had garage sales year round! For those you live and in climates where the winners are harsh, it's probably your best bet to have your sales during the spring summer and fall. **Unless you have a heated barn… just saying! If you have it, they will come!**

As you get ready for your first sale this is going to be the most challenging one for you! By following the procedures laid out in this book after your first sale you'll be more than a third of the way ready for your next sale.

That is why I said put the price that you want to receive on your nicer items and stick to it, within reason. **Example- if you are asking $400.00 and they offer you $370.00, take the money and say thank you! Losing $370.00 to make $30.00 is crazy!** The philosophy is this your first sale not your last sale which gives you a piece of mind. **If it doesn't sell this time it will sell the next time.** The longest it took me to sell an item was three garage sales.

Most stuff will sell in the first two garage sales. You already have your storage place setup, all of the items are already priced this just a matter of putting it back into your storage spot and waiting for the time that you can have your next garage sale. **Now you see the point of all that hard work and preparation. There is a method to the madness!**

Hot damn!

Now you have a new problem where do I get more merchandise? Now, that you are a seasoned garage sale veteran, well after this sale you will be.

You now know what to look for at other garage sales that will make you money! Most garage sales are poorly executed, hence the reason that they do not make a lot of money. I had one close friend tell me she made $280 on a three days garage sale. I did not have the heart to tell her that on my last garage sale **I made more that that before 12:00 PM on the first day!**

To some this may seem unethical, to go out and get great deals at other garage sales. Not even close! This is the United States of America where the smart survive and the not so smart…well you know the deal.

They had the same opportunity to buy this book that you did so is 100% fair. After you had your sale and you go to someone else's garage sale, you'll see so many things that are wrong it will drive you crazy… until you start snapping up the deals to be had, at this not so well organized garage sale. You will have numerous opportunities to do this; you will find yourself becoming super picky. The reason

The Ultimate Garage Sale / 55

behind this is you have 20 or more garage sales to attend and out that 20, 15 or more are not come to be as good as yours was!

Now this is the point that you're about to become a totally different garage sale person. Understand, that those other garage sale hosts do not have information that you have. Ask for discount, ask if you'll give a discount for buying in volume, and ask for things that you do not see.

Unlike your sale, a great many garage sales are thrown together at the very last minute. Frequently, there are items still in the house that they did not bring out for the sale that they did not have the time to bring out for display. **I scored 300 CDs this way!**

I was chatting up the host the garage sale and I noticed that she did not have any music outside. I ask her if she had any CDs for sale. She said "oh yes!" There all in this box it's too heavy for me to move. I asked her if she minded if I went inside to look over the CDs. She told me where they were and she would give me a discount if I brought the box outside for her. **(Yes, some people will let you into their homes; I cannot tell you how many times this has happened to me)** Once I saw the CDs I wanted them all, they were in pristine condition. I made sure all the CDs were in the jewel cases **(you always have to check for that, people leave CDs in the weirdest of places)** I offered her $80 for the box; she said if I can do $100 I had myself a deal. That was 30¢ per CD, because there were some limited edition and rare CDs in the box, **I made well over $950 off that buy!** This happens every day of the summer when people are having garage sales. The deals are out there you just got to ask for what you want.

Also reframe your mindset; you're a buyer not a seller. This is really huge in terms of scoring great items for your garage sale. **TIP!** Ask the sellers if they have any gold in the house, you might be pleasantly surprised at how much jewelry that people have just laying around that they'll really do not care about. In one word of caution, if you are not really familiar with gold buy yourself the testing kit, you can buy one on eBay for $25.00 well worth the investment. It's acid in real gold will not be dissolved by the acid.

An Open Mouth Gets Feed!-Spread the Word Man!!!

You have got to share the love! Marketing and advertising are the lifeblood of any business or endeavor. This is the secret ingredient to a successful and very profitable garage sale. The more people that know about your garage sale, the better!

I cannot overstate the importance of a great marketing plan and its affect on your garage sale. **This is the whole nine yards and a bag of chips...with the grape soda.** When you get this part right that is when you'll have cars lined up and down the street. This will only draw more people to garage sale because everyone will want to know what is going on why are there so many people there, what is the big deal!

Should you or should you not place a newspaper ad?

In the age of the Internet **newspaper ads or like the dodo bird and dinosaurs, a dying breed.** However, in certain situations there is value in a newspaper ad. If you're having an estate sale and you know the rules about estate sales you need to be selling everything.**(I keep repeating this, because some people are going to try to get away with, call their garage sale an estate sale!)** A newspaper ad will help you. As hard as it is to believe, there are many people that do not the utilized the vast power of the Internet. **It is also a good ideal to use newspaper ads if they are free.** If there is a cost I would not place a newspaper ad. For my tastes they are just not that effective. Many people do not even read the newspapers anymore. So unless is free or you're having an estate sale I was stay far away from newspaper ads.

Social networking is the bomb!

Facebook is a world unto itself, sometimes you learn more about a person on Facebook then you actually do talking to them. That is the power of this platform. You will use the power of social networking resources in promoting your garage sale.

I have seen people place an item or two on Facebook and not really harness all power of that portal. Twitter is also a great resource if you have a lot of local followers that is the key. If most of your followers are all over the world than it's going to be a wash. **Social networking definitely should have a place in your marketing plan.** You will not start advertising your garage sale until a few days before the actual date because of the speed of social networking. Create an event post on your **Facebook** page and link it to your **www.evite.com** account, if you don't have one, no problem. It is quick and easy to sign up and it is free! You will send out the invitations to your garage sale a few weeks in advance. This way as the sale date gets closer, you can send out email reminders to keep your folks in the loop!

Craigslist is my B&^%$!

I absolutely love Craigslist! I have made so much money off of Craigslist it should be a crime! Craigslist even has a special section for garage sales. I'm going to show you a technique that help me generate **$1350** at my first garage sale. I got a ton of compliments about that technique and several phone calls. Advertising your garage sale is what is going to make your sale or break your sale, even if you screw everything else up that's just how powerful advertising is!

Things to include in Your Ad

Whether you're running a newspaper ad or Internet at there's critical elements that need to be present in any situation.

- **Highlight all of your name brand and big ticket items first.**

- **Anything that you have in large quantities put that in the ad also.**

- **An address link from MapQuest or Google maps to your house. Make it as easy as possible for people to get your garage sale.**

- **Place in the ad exact dates and times of your garage sale.**

- **Pictures of the nicest stuff you have.**

- **Give your ad body; make it longer in more detail than the others.**

- **Use capital letters Bold print and big language (Huge, Awesome, Large)**

- **Put your personality into the ad, have fun with it.**

- **Do not lie about what you have or the condition of it tell the truth and make a lot of money!**

Since you are a smart cookie and you're now harnessing the power of the net and social networking here are a few hints to help you make even more successful. You are going to run your ad more than once. **Three days before the sale you are going to run your ad, the day before and the date of the sale very early in the morning you going to run it again! This would be only on Craigslist, not the other sites.**

One of the downsides to the Internet is an overload of information and people's attention spans are not as long as they used to be. To capture those eyeballs you have to be in front of those eyes constantly. During your sale at the midway point on the first day you are going to run your ad again!

Politeness Note- Delete the stuff that sold from fresh ads, people will always want what has already sold!

When you run you're ad early people that catch it late they think all of good stuff is gone and will not even drive to your sale. By placing multiple ads you give your garage sale certain **"freshness"** by employing this technique I kept

a crowd in the garage at all times. There were always 5 to 10 cars outside and that just draws more people.
Do not give out handbills or fliers this only pisses as people off. Back in the day they use to work and worked well that is no longer the case.

Online Ad Examples
THE MOTHER OF ALL GARAGE SALES
Sept 9-11th 8A-4P all days!
We have 1000 of items and we are making
Deals! Furniture, appliance, clothes you name it
we are selling it!
1250 Mockingbird Lane
Atlanta GA 303030
404 404 4040
Check out the photos here www.mygargaeale.com a www.thisisthewaytomyhouse.com

**** DO NOT USE THIS AD UNLESS YOU HAVE 1000S OF ITEMS!*****

1250 Mocking Bird Lane
Atlanta GA 30303
404 404 4040
HUGE GARAGE SALE RAIN OR SHINE
Accent items, rugs, clothing, shoes, saddles, golf clubs
Sporting good, basketball goal, Honda motorcycle this is not
Your mother's garage sale!
Check out the photos here www.mygaragesale.com a www.thisisthewaytomyhouse.com

MOVING AND IT ALL HAS TO GO ESTATE SALE
1250 Mocking Bird Lane
Atlanta GA 30303
404 404 4040
Bedroom furniture, living room furniture, dining room furniture
Rugs, art, pool table, nice grill, chandelier, three big screen televisions
Pottery, pots and pans, high end chef knives, crystal, over 3000 books
Over 1000 CDs and dvds, squat rack, dumbbells, Olympic set,
Very nice office furniture, filing cabinets, bookcases, collectables
Essentially I am selling everything in the house!
Check out the photos here www.myestatesale.com a www.thisisthewaytomyhouse.com

This was my ad when I moved, made $12,000 at the end of the sale! All this stuff came out of storage units! I literally sold everything it took me all week! The only thing I moved was my clothes. (I already had another place which was furnished; I like to change it up!) This was the only six day sale that I ever had. As you can see there's a lot of flexibility in how you do your ad.

If you noticed, I always included a phone number as well as a map this is critical. Everyone doesn't have GPS and GPS is not always reliable. You want to make it as tremendously easy as possible for that person to attend your garage or estate sale and this is how you do it.

If you're a seasoned garage sale buyer, you know 90% of the garage sale ads do not have a phone number. These people do not want to be bothered with making money! There so many things that can happen where a buyer would truly need your phone number. The biggest reason I always included a phone number was for people that got to the ad late.

The number one phone call that I got, "do you still have the item?" if I had it, **I would say yes and give them a limited time to come get it.** No more than 30 minutes. Unless they were really far away, I would give them more time. Chances are, if someone is driving an hour or more to come get one of your items, it is a done deal. I never had one of those people no go through with the deal in over 8 years! That is just too far to be playing around!

If they say something like okay I'll stop by then sell it to the first person that puts money in your palm. They are not that serious.

Serious people say things like "I am about to head out the door right now!" "Don't sell it I want it" "that's exactly what I've been looking for!"

If you don't hear excitement and enthusiasm in their voice more than likely they are not that **interested** in your item. They may have a strong curiosity, but not strong enough to grab the cash and hit the road! Just keep moving forward with your sale, but remain polite and friendly at all times!

Sometimes you can turn these warm leads into cold hard cash! You already have their name and number; just write it down before you get off the phone, along with the item they expressed an interest. Call them back if it doesn't sell,

60% of the time they say no, but you will convert some of them.

 Therefore you will not hold it. Keep it on a business tip; remember your ultimate goal is to make as much money as possible from your garage sale. Not to make friends! Having your phone number in the ad may enable you to make big sales before the sale.

During your garage sale day prep week, you are a selling machine you're in the mode and you should be open to any and all sales.

Example-you just placed your ad 30 minutes later you get a phone call, the caller states, I want that item I will come get it now! When people say things like that and do not **haggle about price is best to strike when the iron is hot!**

This will happen! I know I have made more money by having the phone number in my garage sale did then leaving it out. Many deals were done before the person arrived. We agreed to price and they showed up with the cash and a truck.

Safety Tip- if you are home alone, get a neighbor to come over or set up the time to met when you are not alone, better to be safe than sorry. I have never had any "incidents on Craigslist in 8 years, but I want you to safe!

The $1350 method

This is what I did; you will need a Gmail account to accomplish this. Once you sign up for a Gmail account if

The Ultimate Garage Sale / 65

you don't already have one that is. (like who doesn't have a Gmail account these days, I actually got my first one off, of Craigslist in the free section!) Log on to your Gmail account and hit the **more** drop down menu

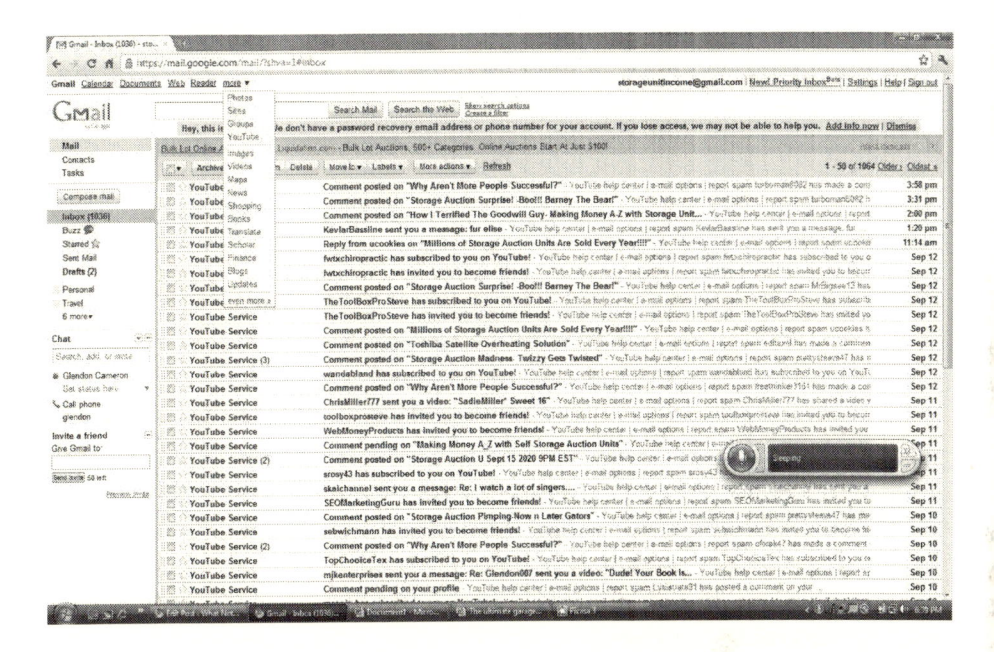

If you have a brand new Gmail account you will be enabling a new **Picasa Web Album** it is very simple. I was the first one to use this method and advertise my garage sale this way on Craigslist's Atlanta. I was truly blown away by the results. My phone was ringing off the hook and people were leaving detailed messages if I did not answer!

On the day of my sale at 7:30 AM I had 20 cars on the street waiting for the garage sale to begin! I've had really good garage sales before this but none like this one. It's going to take a little work to set it up, but it is so worth it!

The Ultimate Garage Sale / 67

The items below were from my thrift store, it works well for personal and business applications!

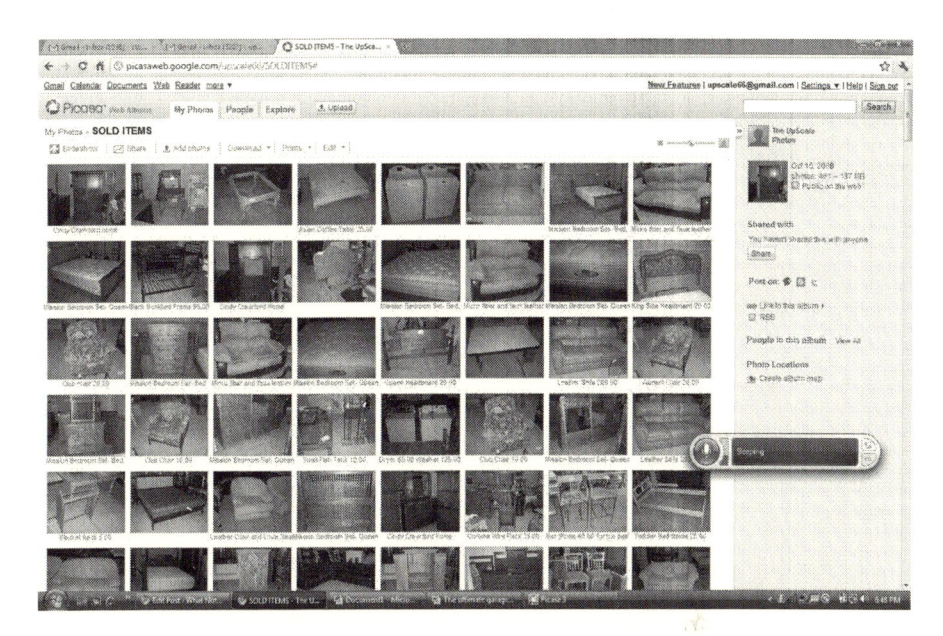

After you have all of Gmail settings done (**you want to use the same Gmail account for your Craigslist ad**) and your Picasa album set up, now is time to take pictures.

You do not have to take a picture of everything. I did take a picture of everything, which resulted in 300, 400, or even 600 pictures once! I grouped some things together, the nicer items I let stand alone in a picture.

The Picasa album allows you to put in the description and price and your buyer can also enlarge the picture for greater detail. This sometimes actually sells the item for you. It's a great resource. Once you have all your pictures uploaded and all the captions and pricing done Picasa album gives you a nifty link that you can put into your online ad.

This one method I would say was extremely valuable and helped me earn more money than I normally would have made, the best things about this it's totally free.

You can have unlimited numbers of pictures. With this method you have a picture of the item already if it doesn't sell. What I would do is delete the items that sold and repost the ad with a fresh link every few hours. This gave me a steady flow of traffic. Nothing makes people stop at a garage sale like a street full of cars! It is very simple just takes a little time a camera and a plan.

Setting Up Your Sale (your time to shine!)

Depending on where you going to have your sale determines what type of prep work you going to do for the space, where you will hold your sale.

If your sale was going to be inside your home or the basement prepping will be at a minimum. If it's going to be in your garage as a few things need to be done first.

You're going to need to enlist the aid of others on this one, if your garage is particular messy! Set a day aside for this project, you will take everything out of the garage. You probably going to find some more stuff to sell at your garage sale that you completely forgot about.

Yes the garage has many secrets and on this day all will be exposed. This will be a lot of work the first time you do it, you may need to take a weekend to get this done.

After you get everything out of the garage, you want to remove all of the debris, trash and unattractive items that are in your garage. Once everything is out depending upon how bad the floor is, you can scrub it down or rinse it off. A clean garage is inviting it will make you more money, trust me on this. Wipe down the shelves the racks and give everything a good cleaning. The fact that your garage is clean and smells nice will make you stand out from other garage sales and your customers will tell you about it!

This may be a chore within itself, but is something that you probably need to do anyway and the motivation of making money will spur you onto getting it done. During your garage sale anything that you were not planning on selling needs to be removed are covered up. **Once you garage sale is underway, folks will want to buy anything they see or can get their hands on!** An ounce of prevention is worth a pound of cure. You're going to have so much going on with your garage sale, the less distractions that you have the better off that you will be.

Kid Note- If you have same children it is best to have someone watch them during your sale. It will be easier on you and the little ones!

Let's talk about layout, on the next page there is a general theme that you can follow. Understand that everyone doesn't have the same space or house so you can make modifications. Here are some hard and fast rules.

You want to have bookcases, shelves and racks along the walls; they are thinner and hold a lot of stuff. I would keep the clothing racks inside next to wall that saved me a lot of pain and effort.

I always kept the clothing close to the cash out table. Buyers often have a lot of questions about clothing. Other things that I also kept close by, were the more expensive items or things that kids will want to play with. A good rule of thumb is to you have the toys out of the reach of little kids.

You will want your aisles as wide possible based on the space that you were dealing with. Some of your customers are going to be wider than others; **(not hating, just stating!)** you want your customers to be comfortable. The more comfortable that they are, the more money that they will spend. By making your garage sale inviting and a pleasure to attend people will tell other folks about your garage sale. **I've had people leave and come back with friends!** The setup is crucial to your success and you'll hear over and over again I've never been to a garage sell so well organized.

These are few suggestions-

You can make tables out of boxes of the same height or place a board over two chairs and cover it with a sheet or blanket. Make sure that your makeshift tables are close to the wall. Any tables that you make up boxes that are sturdy

Any electronic items that you're trying the sell, televisions and computers, **I mean anything that powers up should be on.** This is a garage sale, this is a used item, and people are very leery about buying something that does not work.

To put them at ease immediately, just have all electronic items on or playing this shows them it works and it saves you from explaining if it works or not. Believe or not, many people will not ask you to turn something on or what the price of an item is. They would just leave your garage sale wondering if it works!

If you have any of the original packaging for any item along with the manual or instructions include those things in your garage sale. It is definitely a winning touch, whenever I recycled my laptops on eBay or Craigslist I always had the box the manuals and CDs, these few things always got me my asking price. **Because 98% of the other people selling laptops did not have these things!**

If you are a storage auction person, you want to have business cards printed up and a emailing list signup sheet. True garage sale veterans will love it. Just let them know they'll be the first people to know about any new stuff that you get. Everyone wants to be first!

This time put on your Ranger hat, always be prepared. Like any good garage sales pro you will check the weather before the day of the sale. However, Mother Nature has a will of her own. So, it is best if you can get everything in your garage. If you have a tremendous amount of stuff that isn't going to work, Home Depot and Lowe's sell large plastic tarps to cover up whenever you have outside very quickly. Often showers come and go, it is best to be prepared. Buy more if you are having your sale outside!

Make sure everything is clean! This will get you extra money! I know it can be a pain but this will be the difference between getting $5.00 for an item or $ 15.00! A shiny item draws attention, it is worth the effort.

I used white sheets to cover my tables (I bought a unit that had over 5000 sheets in it) whatever you use, make sure it is clean! Use old blankets, quilts, drapes anything that will cover the tables. Make sure they smell fresh there is nothing like a funky smell to chase folks out of your garage!

Use large colorful signs to identify the nicer and larger items; you can print them up on your computer in no time. Anything to draw more attention to your items is well worth the printer ink! I found out using colored paper, worked very well at drawing attention to the higher priced items!

Be sure to have your check out area at the entrance that way you can greet people as they come and collect the cash as they leave.

You can be very creative with this, as long as the tables are sturdy and do not tip over you are good to go. You can borrow tables from friends are by a few pieces of plywood place heavy boxes at each end and covered with a sheet or blanket. I use layout on the next page, in my two car garage and in my basement when I had the estate sale.

You're going to have your bookcases shells and racks along the walls and you may want to invest in clothing racks. **They're very inexpensive and all male and female: should be hung on a rack.** This will keep them from being wrinkled and scattered all over the place. Make sure that you have male and female clothing on separate racks. Kids' clothing can go in a box, and usually there will be a lot more kids' clothing than adult.

Just check for sales or try Big Lots they always have a deal. The general theme that you wanted to be is clean and attractive. Those two factors alone will separate you from other garage sales. Having all of your items priced, in order and well laid out will make your money.

The Ultimate Garage Sale / 74

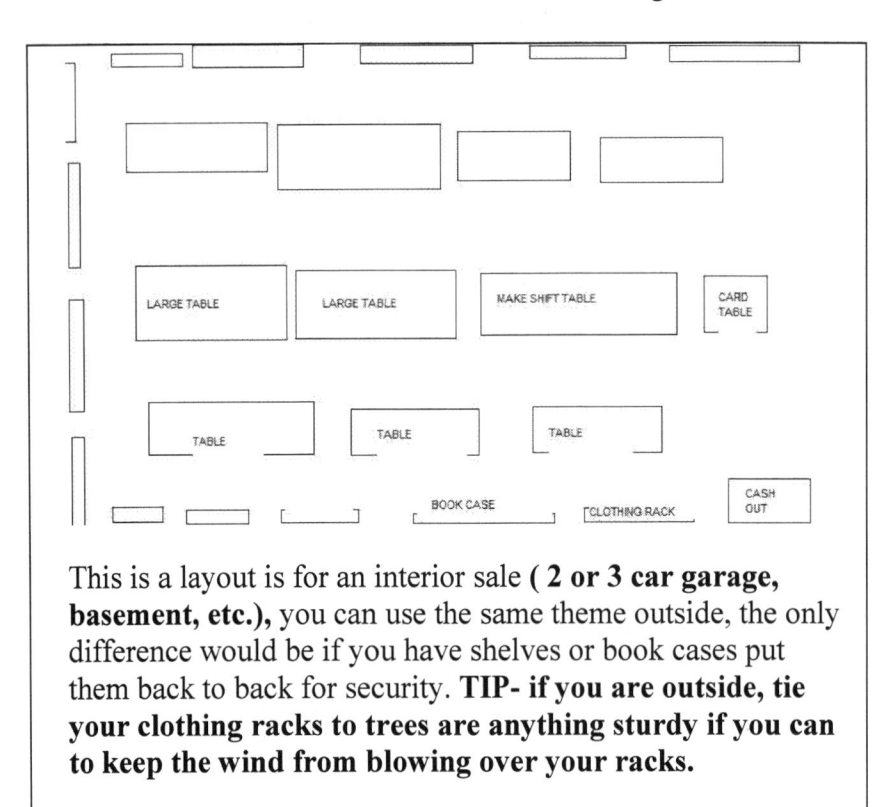

| LARGE TABLE | LARGE TABLE | MAKE SHIFT TABLE | CARD TABLE |

| TABLE | TABLE | TABLE |

BOOK CASE   CLOTHING RACK   CASH OUT

This is a layout is for an interior sale **(2 or 3 car garage, basement, etc.),** you can use the same theme outside, the only difference would be if you have shelves or book cases put them back to back for security. **TIP- if you are outside, tie your clothing racks to trees are anything sturdy if you can to keep the wind from blowing over your racks.**

Garage Sale Signs (Home Made Are the Best!)

This is a major part of your advertising effort for your garage sale. Signage is very important. **If you come away with nothing else from this book, please understand I can not over emphasize this enough. Signs to your garage sale are like oxygen to lungs.**

GARAGE SALE

This is a good sign, yet there are a few problems. Number one the sign is too small. **(It is 11 x 11)** Have you ever been looking for a garage sale only to find yourself squinting to look at the sign?

Remember my mantra no one's going to work hard to spend money! Your signs should be huge and simple.

And once again looking to sign above, if it was larger it would be perfect. With the addition of an address, dates and times.

You do not want a lot of stuff going on with your sign. **When people are driving they're going to see your sign for just a few seconds.** You have a very small window of opportunity to reel them in.

What you want is a very good contrast; **I find the neon or fluorescent colors of yellow, orange, green, and pink work very well with a high contrast letter scheme.** What you want to include is the pertinent information of your garage sale. The fact that you have a garage sale, date and time and the address, all of this information should be clearly legible and in large print. Clarification- Your main theme –Ex- The Upscale Garage Sale can and should be larger than the body with location details, that is the hook. Once you have their attention, they need a clear message that points them to your sale!

All of your signs should have the same *color and letter scheme*. This is super important! **Having great garage sale signs will make or break your garage sale this can be the difference between absolutely stunning success or just making a few dollars.** I have bought signs from the store, **this has been my experience that home made signs work the best and their cheaper.** Home Depot and Lowes even have wooden stakes for signs now in the wood section.

Use a heavy duty stapler to affix the signs to the post, so you do not wear out your hand on getting your signs ready!

Starting about a mile away from your home, you want to put your signs on every corner and cross street all of the way to your house. This is one of the things that drives me absolutely bonkers, with some other garage sales!

You see one or two signs and on your way to the garage sale and you can't find the sale! I can't recall how many times this happened to me! I am driving around, going one or two streets over and I still cannot find that blank-blank garage sale! You don't want to be this person, think back to bread crumbs.

Your mission here is to ensure that buyers make it to your garage sale with the least difficulty possible. This is fundamentally critical to your success; do not skimp on the signs. Your signs are your garage sale's representative. Over the years I have learned that the best signs are indicative of the best garage sales.

My thoughts on preprinted signs

Don't do it, I know that they make it easy to just buy a sign and throw it up. However, you are not looking for easy you are looking to make a substantial profit from your garage sale! To make the most money with a garage sale you need to make an impact and you have greater creative control and license with your own signs.

Most preprinted signs in my opinion are too small. Large fluorescent cardboard poster board is very economical and

The Ultimate Garage Sale / 78

so are the markers. I suggest getting the big jumbo markers; please use in a well ventilated area! I have bought brand new signs and I have had some made up to my specifications, read that as very large!

The signs that I had custom made worked very well. So well in fact, that people stole those signs!

I actually drove up to a garage sale that was using one of my custom signs and I repossessed my sign. The people at the garage sale said that it just blew into the yard. (Insert side eye) Right, sure it did.

That is one of the biggest risks that you have when you use fancy signs. Not to mention if the sign is hand made and stolen it is not that big of a loss. My custom signs were **$30.00** each! I had **25** made and lost **5** on the first garage sale that I used them!

Over the course of three sales I lost over half of those signs! I was hopping mad! Yes, the signs worked like a charm! But do this at your own risk, just know in advance that fancy, super nice custom garage sale signs will be stolen, and yes they will do it during your sale!

Sign Patrol!

During your sale you want to enlist the aid of a sign rover that will check you signs ever hour on the hour to make sure the wind doesn't blow them down or that someone did not make off with any of your signs! In some places, Code Enforcement personnel will pull them up; if they are in places they should not be, such as telephone poles, close to fire hydrates. That is why I say have a few extra signs on hand.

This is a, <u>don't</u> on the streets; can work on the mailbox of your home. It is too small!

The Ultimate Garage Sale / 80

What the hell is going on here?

The Ultimate Garage Sale / 81

Just say no to pack! Too small and coded colored labels can help induced deception!

The Ultimate Garage Sale / 82

Cute but waaaaaaay too small!

The Ultimate Garage Sale / 83

The only good one is the large white sign, think large and clear. Remember your customers are driving!

Ahhh.... so close but so far away the size is right but the execution sucks!

The Ultimate Garage Sale / 85

What the hell? You get the gas face my man! The one below is "creative" but wrong as hell! Imagine if you saw this driving 35-45mph?

The Ultimate Garage Sale / 86

> Snakes on a Garage Sale
>
> Our Summertime
> Mondo
> BIG ASS Sale
>
> This Saturday only (8/19/06)
> 9am & on well into the afternoon
>
> 1379 10th Avenue @ Judah Street
>
> ...struction supplies, Huge Mirrors, Video Games
> Collectables, Kitchenware, Furniture, Clothes
> ...tronics, Movies, Music, Bevies and the like

Damn! So close! If the background was high contrast, print larger, this would be a winner! It has all of the pertinent information. I give it a B- !

The Ultimate Garage Sale / 87

Cute but no cigar too small and no contrast!

The Ultimate Garage Sale / 88

Just lean back from your computer screen, can you make it out at 2 feet, now think about looking at from 30 feet away! This is not the time for an art contest!

Works for me! It is large and you can see it from far away, something clear and simple is better than fancy and busy!

I took a lot of time on the signs chapter, because it's super critical to your success. I cannot over emphasize this point. You have been busting your butt to get ready for your garage sale; this is not the time to fall down on the job!

The Winner is! You can't miss this baby; you know this is a serious garage sale!

Sign Checklist!

- ➢ Use large signs, big as you can make them!
- ➢ Florescent colors are best!
- ➢ The "MAIN THEME SHOULD STAND OUT!"
- ➢ Use the same type of letters on all signs, folks are easily confused!
- ➢ Very clear printing "LARGE", do not use cursive writing it can be confusing!
- ➢ Contrasting lettering and background is a must!
- ➢ Included date, time and address
- ➢ Make sure all of the arrows are pointing in the right direction!
- ➢ Take a stapler with you in case the sign comes off the post when you set them up.
- ➢ Start a mile from your home and work your way back right up to your own mailbox, yes you want to have a sign on your mailbox or entrance way!
- ➢ Steer away from preprinted signs, not as effective as home made! Be creative!
- ➢ Make extra signs in case of wind or theft!

- Have a rover check on your signs during the sale!

- Conduct a test run after you placed your signs out, if you have issues so will your customers!

- I have used a large blow up decoration to advertise my sale, so just maybe those lawns Christmas ornaments can have another purpose!(Note I only used this method at my house!)

- Be sure to gather all of your signs once the sale is over! I would pick up the sign each night and placed them back in the morning.

- Ask permission before placing a sign in someone else's yard! This usually will be a corner location.

- Do not skimp on your signs, this will make or break your sale!

Your Day Of Reckoning! (Cash, Cash, Cash, Cash!)

This is the moment that you have been working so hard for. I always got up early on a garage sale day and had breakfast. Once you start rolling, you're not going to have time for anything other than taking care of your customers. People will start showing up as soon as you place the very first sign out! Some people would place them out the night before; I liked placing them out the day of the sale. It is a personal preference.

I always had help with my garage sales; you'll need someone to be there with you for bathroom breaks, lunch and to watch the crowd. If you have a lot of stuff three to four people will be required.

If you've never have a really busy garage sale, it can overwhelm you! This is a good thing, that's why it pays to be prepared. This is the mindset that I have; people waiting are people that have money that they want to give to me!

At every garage sale that is well advertised, you will have early birds. This could be a good thing or bad thing. I always make sure everything was set up and ready to go before placing out the first sign. And I had my help in the garage waiting on the customers to come in. It usually starts off very fast sometimes there is a rush and other times they come in waves. It's just the best to be ready for them before you place your signs out.

No Garage! So it is a Yard Sale Man!

For those of you who do not have a garage, this will be a different drill for you! The set up can be the same, except you will be getting up at **0 dark thirty** to get ready for your sale. The night before you can set up all of the tables and racks, in the morning just place the stuff out on the tables. I would advise having as much help as possible during this stage! If you followed my advice about pricing your items as you stored them away in preparations for the sale **50% of your work is already done!**

Some adventurous folks will set up everything the night before and place tarps over everything that is up to you! It really depends on your neighborhood. If it was me, I would not do it!

To each, his own as my grand dad would say, use a room close to the door you will be using the most to set up outside, as a staging room in the house.

It is far easier to move stuff out of one room to the outside versus bring stuff from all over the house! You will also have a place to bring the stuff back in once the sale concludes for that day!

Dealing with early birds

This is your sale you can conduct it anyway that you wish, how ever the goal is to make as much money as possible. Early birds are usually the diehard garage sale veterans, people with a lot to do that day, the super curious and deal hunters (read store owners) they will spend money. There are different schools of thoughts about this; I look at it from this point of view. If you have a store with customers begging to get in wouldn't you open up early to let them in?

 If you are a progressive merchant of course you would! Why should a garage sale be any different? Like I said before this is your garage sale and you can run it anyway that you choose. **Just know that you stand the chance of losing money by not addressing these people.**

It is best to be totally set up and ready to go with your garage sale before you go to bed that night. By utilizing the rules in this book you will be ahead of the average bear. Thus, this should not be a problem. In life things happen and we must adjust. **I would let them in and start taking their money as soon as possible!**

 Usually they will sit in their cars on the street and wait for you to start. Most people are very pleasant and considerate it when it comes to this, yet there are some people that will test you.

Be polite yet firm and tell them you will let them know when the sale will start if you're not ready. I have had some very aggressive people come to my garage sales. If they know that you're not playing they will fall in line. Some people as soon as they see any hint of activity in your garage , will jump out of their cars and pounce on your garage sale. Like a hungry cat on a mouse, yes, it is just that serious!

Time For Change

The strangest thing happen to me on my first garage sale, I had a lady spend $5.00 and pay me with $100 bill! So in a word you should be prepared for all contingencies.

This is a breakdown of the money I had on hand to make change at my garage sales. I had $100 in $20.00 bills, $25.00 in $5.00 bills, $30.00 in $10.00 bills, $35.00 in $1.00 bills. I did not have that much change, to accomplish this are priced items at a dollar or more, I never had problem with this method.

I'd take that back older people or the elderly will have change! Even with that many $1.00 bills on occasion I still ran out! It is better have more change than you need than to not have enough. **Money Tip! When making change, always keep the bill that was giving to you in plain sight while you make change, only after the deal is done do you put the money in your pocket!** This keeps the unethical from trying to take advantage of you! No one can say I gave you a $50.00 when in fact they gave you a $20.00!

On your checkout this table you will have your change box, a notebook-**this is what you going to record your sales tally in.** Your newspaper to wrap fragile items in plus your bags for your customers to carry their newly bought treasures home in. If you do not feel comfortable having a change box, wear an apron. You can pick up a contractor's apron or carpenter's apron fairly cheaply. With all those pockets, you have a place for the cash your notebook on you. I recommend the apron if you're conducting the garage sale by yourself, just one less thing to worry about.

Have you ever noticed that in any store that you have entered, they are playing music? Do the same at your garage sale, I find older songs to be the best choice, contemporary, R&B or pop music to be widely admired. It sets a nice tone for your garage sale. This is also a great way to showcase any of the stereo equipment that you're selling. Once you sell your electronic items just to have a small radio to keep the mood going. Nine times out of ten, the stereo will be one of the first things to go!

A Few Precautions You Should Take!

This may come to you as a shock, it's a very sad fact of life, but people steal from garage sales!

Yes, it is a trip! These are some tips that you can use to prevent this are the least cut down on the theft that occurs at your garage sale. It's an obvious step to watch your money at all times.

 I strongly encourage you to keep your money on your person. Once the cash bundle becomes too large, just have someone take the large bills inside of the house. Just keep enough on you to make change. No need for people to see how much money you are making!

Here is a small list of high theft items, **CDs, DVD's, video games, jewelry, small items, watches, rings, very nice women's shoes.** I once noticed a pair of dirty run over shoes in the place of some very nice shoes, the perp tried the shoes on and liked them so much, that she walked out with them on! Remember that scene from the *"Shawshank Redemption?"* Where Andy is walking out with the warden shoes? She must have seen it too! These are the items that I had the most problems with!

It is best to keep these items close to the checkout table or you make a point to stay close to the table with these items on it. This is why it is important for you to have assistance at your garage sale. That occurs when you're very busy; this gives the perpetrator a window of opportunity to make off with your stuff.

Watch out for a group of people huddled around the table and no one's asking you questions. Not always, but in some cases they are using the bodies of their friends as a shield, giving the thief cover. Is always a good idea to have someone constantly walking around the sale, this keeps people honest.

On **Craigslist** there is a section under services were you can find people that offer the service of moving and delivering. This is a wonderful resource for your larger items, solving the dilemma of delivery sometimes will close the sale!

Actually put this in your ad, that you have options available for delivery. Many single women, especially if their new to the area do not have help to move large items. If it's something really nice, say in the neighborhood of $500 to $1000 you can include the cost to delivery in the price. On this deal, if they haggle I would take delivery off of the table unless their substantial profit still in it even coming down a few points.

If you're selling computers, video games, very nice stereo systems, televisions or any other nice electronic item, you want to place these items out of the reach of children. **Do not expect their parents to watch them.** This is where having help also comes into play people are going to bring kids to your garage sale. Better to be prepared for them than to hope they will not come.

To generate a More Loot At Your Sale!

If you are a Mary Kay or Avon representative just set up a table with your merchandise this is a great way to grow your client list. A friend of mine set up at one of my garage sales with her Mary Kay samples and signed up 35 new regular customers at one garage sale!

If it is hot, sell bottled water and freeze pops, you can buy both at Sam's Club or Wal-Mart in bulk very economically!

Sell cookies, candy or baked goods, the crowd is there, they will buy!

I would be careful with food, most places it is illegal to sell food without a permit. Yes, I know people do it all of the time!

There are many ways to enhance the profits of your garage sale! Thanks for reading! If you are a storage auction buyer I got something special for you in the next chapter!

Storage Auction Addicts this is for You!

I wrote this book with the average person in mind first and the storage auction buyer second. Because it's all going to be the same until you get to the sourcing of inventories, in terms of preparation, set up, marketing, your garage sale signs, and things to watch out for when hosting your sale.

Tip For Storage Auction Buyers!

If you are a storage auction unit buyer, there are going to be some remarkable differences between what you would do and the average person just holding a garage sale. **I highly suggest that you have your own personal garage sale before you start buying units and try to sell the stuff in your home! You will need the space!**

Because if you just get into the storage auction business before you prep your house your home will be overflowing with stuff. You need to have a method to help you with the madness.

This step is actually in my first book *Making Money A-Z with Self Storage Auction Units- The Black Edition* when

I was so deep in the storage auction business it took two years for me clean out my house! You can get so much stuff out of a storage unit ***it can and will take over your home***, if you do not have a great game plan on your auction inventory management systems. I will share this with you; you can have a better Monday than most people's Christmas with the storage auction lifestyle!

We are going to start from the standpoint that your house is already free clear of clutter and you can just have a garage sale. When you buy storage unit, there is no telling what you going to come across. That is part of the thrill of storage auction units, you can win big!

One key difference between you and the average garage sale host is the fact that you will be keeping up with your customers. At each of your sales, you will have an **e-mail signup sheet and business cards. You want to be sure to capture the customer's full name, e-mail address and phone number. Going forward this list, will become a license to print money!**

An excel spread sheet will work perfectly in the beginning, if your client list becomes large, you may want to purchase a copy of ACT or Goldmine, these are CRM –customer relationship management software packages.

Both are nifty tools and very robust. When I was in Corporate America I took a week long class to learn how to use Goldmine. Don't worry, for your uses it will take you about 15 minutes to learn how to operate it.

Repeat customers will become your best friends and move your business forward like you would not believe! The building of a client list is super important. After a few months, your customers will start calling you inquiring about specific items.

You want to have a job book are customer book where you will write down these requests. When you see it in the unit, you can buy it and know it is already sold. When you work your customer list in this method, your clients will start to spread the word.

For every one customer that you sign up, over the course of the year that can matriculate into 3 to 6 more new customers! Now, that's a new kind of math, I know you will love! This is the value of great customer service and building your client list. By doing this you become a valuable resource in their lives. Many of my customers actually became friends!

I know one storage auction buyer that does not even have sales; she attends auctions looking for the specific items for her customers. I wholesaled a lot of items to her. There are many ways that you can make money was storage unit auctions.

The Four House Boogie

This is a strategy for the very bold, and the person that has a lot of really good friends. In most municipalities, you're only allowed to have four garage sales a year. This could be very problematic if you want to hold one every month. If you are in one of those places no one cares, then go for it! Have as many garage sales as you can!

However, after doing your due diligence, you find out that you cannot have a lot of garage sales. The follow method will work for you. This is a legal way to stay within the letter of the law.

You are going to recruit three other house wholes to help you with your business. You will be responsible for all permits, license and cleanup. You'll make enough money that you can just give them say the $100 or $150 for the use of their garage. In most cases, when they see how much money you're making they will want to participate. Do not say that I did not warn you!

It may not be a bad ideal to partner up, but if you were going to be partners, you will be full partners. This means everyone has skin in the game. They need to put money up if they want to be involved in your storage auction business.

As a storage auction buyer, you will have access to more inventory than the average person. This is awesome! Your challenge will be, creating systems and processes to efficiently buy and sell your merchandise.

Let's start with the easy stuff. There will be some storage auction units, that you can load, price and present for your garage sale immediately. **Do not count on this being the case that most of the time!**

Many of the items will have to be sorted, inventoried, researched, cleaned up and then you can set them up for sale. If you bought my first book *Making Money A-Z with Self Storage Unit Auctions The Black Edition* you will have at a minimum of three selling channels. Thus, the sorting and research process should not be an onerous one to you.

If you have not read the book, this is the procedure. You are going to have what I call a rolling inventory; take all of items that are easy to identify price wise put them aside for a garage sale. More challenging items or things that you know are valuable; you just don't know how valuable will require more effort and time to determine their market price.

I know the first thought would be to deal with all of the expensive and would be profitable items first. This is where you get into trouble. This leads to what I call **a home run mentality.** You start to seek out these items exclusively and look upon other items that do not bring instant and large profits as a burden. With these blinders on, you will miss out on a lot!

Small items sold in volume can make an amazing amount of money! Just look at McDonalds, they are making millions $5.00 bucks at a time! It adds up and it is more sustainable than concentrating on the larger items all of the time. By working all ends of the market **(low, middle and upper)** you stand a better chance for consistent cash flow, thus constant profits!

It's like taking a standardized test, do the easy stuff first and come back and do the harder stuff later. Once you get some experience under your belt, this will become second nature. Any item that you do not know the value of put aside. You do not have to sell everything at the first garage sale. For you this is going to be an ongoing concern. You well have new inventory coming in every week. This inventory needs to be managed. As you go about buying units at auction there's going to be a great benefit. You are going to get more storage bins/containers than you have ever seen in your life. These bins will help you keep your inventories organized and prepped for sale.

The first time that you put an item up for sale is going to be the hardest. This is what we would call a raw item. Understand that everything will not sell at a garage sale the first time. Do not let that trouble your heart, sometimes item sells for much more when seasons change! At this juncture, you will have a space designated for your garage sale inventories.

Use the larger bins for clothing and the smaller the bins for the heavier the items that you can put into it. I know this goes against popular thinking, many would think cram as much stuff as possible into the larger bins.

This is the fallacy with that train of thought. You going to be moving these bins around a lot, it will be easier to move a smaller tote filled with heavier stuff, than a larger storage bin crammed to the top with heavy items!

There are times giving away stuff for Free will make you money!

Part of the storage auction world is obtaining massive amounts of stuff. There will be occasion, when it is not feasible to sell a certain item. You may already have the item several times over; the price point is just not worth your time or is really not worth selling. There are several channels that you can get rid of the stuff.

The first one is donation to your favorite charity and taking the write off. You can give it to friends, families or even strangers. Yes, even strangers. Craigslist has a section that I love. It is the **Free Section** every Craigslist City has such a section; you can use it to your advantage. If you have a lot of stuff, that you want to get rid of, treat it just like garage sale inventory.

You will not have to price it, but you will need to take a picture of the items you want to get away. Have the stuff looking as nice as it possibly can, well presented, and people will come taken off of your hands.

Include this stuff, in your garage sale ad. Make it very clear, that you're giving away some very good stuff. The pictures help tremendously. You will post a separate ad on the Free **Section** of Craigslist and you will also note all of the free stuff that you're giving away in your garage sale ad. **Be very clear it is on a first come, first serve basis!** Geesh!, it is free, if they does not make them run to their cars nothing else will!

The keys to making sure that this stuff disappears are all in the presentation and pictures. One of the benefits of giving away the stuff is that people who normally would not even attend your garage sale will be their front and center. Some will just come for the free stuff, which is cool they are helping you. Many will also buy stuff at your garage sale which just helps you in making more money. This would be a case of giving away stuff for free that actually helps you make money. **This is a beautiful thing!**

If items are beyond selling, not worth giving away just toss the items.

Christmas 12 Months A Year!
As a storage auction buyer, you're going to get an unbelievable amount of Christmas ornaments, decorations, Christmas trees, and very nice vintage Christmas paraphernalia. Obviously, you cannot sell these types of items year round. (Well you can , but you make more money during the season) So this is what you do, as long as space permits you keep the nicest of the nice. Over the course of the year it will stack up. You can start selling Christmas items around the end of September at the earliest.

Exception- Rare Hallmark Christmas ornaments do well on eBay, year round. I bought a unit, that had over 1500 Hallmark ornaments, some sold for as high as $150.00 on ebay!

You would clearly get rid of any artificial Christmas trees that are incomplete. The same thing goes with Christmas tree stands, decorations and Christmas train sets. This it will be an ongoing situation as you get new stuff you going to have to make room for it and just get rid of the lesser stuff.

Other types of items that you going to get throughout the year that you can't sell at all times of the year, will be winter stuff. Clothing, skis, jackets, hats, gloves and heaters, which are very fast sellers! You want to hold onto all of your heaters until that first really cold morning, at that point you would advertise them in your garage sale, they will sell like hotcakes! Heaters, too many people, are essential and you can get a very good price on a great working heater.

I have gotten some really great ceramic heaters out of storage units. I currently have five that I still used to this day. I have a little one about the size of a football it will heat up a whole of room, it's amazing. Brand new this thing is $150. **I should say, there will be many things that you will keep for your own personal use.** That is one of the greatest benefits of being a storage auction buyer next to the money that you can make. Before long, if you're not already addicted, you will be!

Leather Jackets

Leather jackets are another item that you will get in the spades. You want to be careful with leather; the cheap grades are pretty durable since they are very close to be in plastic anyway. I would hang them up, using nicer hangers with padding until I was ready to sell them. This way all of the wrinkles and creases would come out naturally over time.

The nicer grade of leather, which would be your calfskin and lambskin, treat these jackets with love and care. They stretch and if you use the wrong hangar you will have humps in the shoulders. This is not very attractive when you're asking anywhere from **$50.00 up to $350** for a used leather jacket. It's worth the care of the nicer jackets. If you do not believe that people will pay this much for a **used or pre owned item**, just walk into your local clothing consignment store and check out the prices.

Just as it is prudent to price your items as you store them for a garage sale, the same holds true for your storage auction inventory items. **Example-say you find a pair of nice leather driving gloves just place the gloves in a plastic baggie and put a price on the bag.** They are in a nice presentation situation and are priced.

 You no longer have to deal with them if they sell great you collect the money. If not you just put them away until next time. This makes your business operation more efficiently, and it keeps you from doing the same thing over and over again.

Fake or faux fireplaces sell throughout the year. The same goes with the gas logs or the electric fireplaces that plug into the wall. People really love these fake fireplaces!

If you come across a cast iron stove or what some would call a potbelly stove, they sell your round also. This is a great auction item; they can be hard to find in great condition. So folks snatch them up with a quickness!

The Boots Were Made For Walkin!

Boots are a great seller, especially the ladies boots. You will often get them out of the storage unit in their original box. Hold on to that box, it often has a price tag on it. This will help you get top dollar for those boots. I used to put antifungal spray in all the shoes whether they had a smell or not, this is just a good policy to follow. The spray does not cost that much.

Just let the boots accumulate and you can start selling the boots in September right after Labor Day. I do not care if it's 100°outside, as soon as Labor Day is over the women folk are in their boots, with their tank tops on. This lets you know it is officially boot season. In some parts of the country, people wear boots year round. Let your geographical location determine, when it's the best time for you to make a decision to start selling boots.

Cowboy boots are hot, hot, hot and very expensive! I bought a unit that had over 650 brand new pairs of cowboy boots. Men are little different, they will buy what they need when they need it. But as in the case of the ladies boots use your own good judgment in determining when is a good time to sell your winter merchandise.

Winter Sports Equipment

Equipment such as skis, snowboards and ice skates can be tricky. The reason for this, is somewhere in the world these activities take place every month for the year. I would use this as a benchmark to determine if you going to sell these type of things at your garage sale or not.

I call it the eBay factor. Some brands of skis are ridiculously expensive. They may be worth holding onto until 2 or 2 ½ months just before Christmas. Things like that make great Christmas gifts!

Yes, people will buy Pre owned or used merchandise for Christmas gifts. I did this for years! Believe it or not you can have a garage sale say four weeks before Christmas and do very well if you have super nice stuff. This is about the only time where super nice stuff really comes into play. Or if you have a customer base that you've built up over the months and the e-mail list that you can do in e-mail blast.

You can be selling items right up to maybe three or four days before Christmas.

Anything that is fall or winter related you can sell a month early, before the season. You'll often get more money in the middle of the season because new stores have moved that merchandise out of stock in it is very hard to find.

Such as heaters, big box retailers will start moving these items out of their inventories while it is still very cold. I just don't understand it, but I've never ran a large retail store. I do know that people want heaters 12 months out of the year. Many women have told me they put them under the desks in their offices because the air conditioning is too cold.

I find it best to do one thing at a time at the situation permits. What I mean by this is you're not going to accomplish your tasks by any other means available to you. The way that the auctions are organized, that is going to be the only thing you can do at that time.

So there is acquisition, that's when you're buying your units. After you have bought your units, the next phase is discovery. This is where it all becomes very interesting exciting, once you have ascertain what you have, then you start to funnel those items into your selling channels.

Garage sales are great way to move the pedestrian items that you're going to get out of a storage unit this will include clothing, household items such as cleaner, plungers, detergent, bathroom sets, towels, rags, fans, heaters and other items that are not suitable for online sales.

If you're not a garage sale person then your outlet for this stuff would be the flea market. Many of the same principles that go into having a garage sale apply at the flea market. The fundamental differences will be the scope of your sale and exclusivity.

Having a garage sale is essentially having your own personal flea market; you will gain all the traffic and all of the profits. Flea markets are great and the better ones have a lot of traffic, but you must share that traffic with other flea market vendors. This is not the case with your own garage sale. It is your party, and your party only, it is a case of having your cake and eating it too!

Can I sell Big Tickets Items at A Garage Sale?

Oh yes, you can! I have sold numerous big ticket items at garage sales. Such as **riding lawn mowers, bedroom sets, living room sets, dining room sets, refrigerators, washer and dryer sets, pianos, a 12 foot trailer, motorcycle, go kart, Jet Ski and a Polaris ATV.** The trick to selling big ticket items at garage sales is making your buyers aware that you have these items . In your marketing and advertising efforts, with forms of payment and delivery options, as I said before the fact that you can make this purchase painless aids in you closing the deal!

If you remember where I was described **the best way to meet expectations is to be the architect of those expectations, this is what I'm talking about.** Let's discuss payment of big ticket items. Many people do not have the cash to buy big ticket items but they can't put it on a credit card.

PayPal has several features that allow you to accept payment other than an eBay auction. There is Virtual Terminal, phone payments and e-mail payments. I used to use e-mail payments all of the time. Someone would come to the sale and see a big ticket item that they wanted. Usually there was some discussion with either a parent or spouse and they had a make a phone call.

My pitch would be this, will you can use your credit card I will have to use my PayPal account and you will get a receipt for the purchase. People that really wanted the item always took me up on it.

I would get their e-mail address, login into my PayPal account and send them an invoice. This was done in two different ways, if they had someone at home to make the payment they would complete the transaction and I will get a confirmation e-mail and help them load their purchase.

If they did not have anyone at home, I would open up my Mozilla or Firefox web browser clear all of the cookies out of the cache and let them log into their own PayPal account to confirm the purchase.

A few things to be aware of, PayPal captures all IP addresses and this may trigger a fraud issue, in my case with over hundreds of transactions I never had a problem. I would log into my PayPal account using Internet Explorer (Goggle chrome was not out back then) and made sure that the customer logged into a different browser that was cookie free.

The customers' privacy is also another concern; people are leery about letting a stranger look at their personal information as well as they should be. Before I will let them long on I would get up and let them sit my chair to conduct the transaction with their back to a wall. Once everything was approved I will let them watch me delete the cookies out of my cache, so anything funny happened with their PayPal account they knew it wasn't me.

Computer Note- put a "Not 4 Sale" sign on your laptop that you are using at your garage sale; if you do not at least 30 people will inquire!

It also made them feel better about me as a person to conduct the transaction with, because I've valued their privacy. Some people would come to my sales with no money because they knew I could take a credit card and this actually increased my sales.

When I would conduct a garage sale at my house just to get rid of stuff that I did not feel like a lugging to the store I would bring home my credit card machine. Plug it up and place it on my check out table. I actually sold more stuff that probably normally would have, because of the credit card machine.

Note- I did not use a credit card machine for my estate sale it was cash only. You can still make a lot of money without using a credit card machine; this is just to let you know what your options are.

There will be a fee and a monthly charge of anywhere from $25.00 to $45.00 per month for the service and a per item transaction fee of .25-.32 cents. If you're going to get in the business, it would behoove you to get your own merchant account. You will capture those impulse buys with a credit card machine, it they have to leave to go get the **money there is a 50% chance they will not come back!**

It is true, people spend more money when they have the ability to pay with a credit card are a debit card. The fees on a debit card pin based transaction are lower and in some cases free compared to a credit card based transaction.

Everyone has a debit card these days. If you do sign up for the merchant account**, just accept Visa and MasterCard they are the most common credit/debit cards** and fees for American Express and Discover are higher. Not to mention, only a small segment of society carries a Discover card.

Granted, this is your business and you can accept those other charge cards if you so choose, but I'm telling you is a waste of time and money. Whether, you use those accounts or not there is a monthly fee for just having the account active. Never had a problem only accepting Visa & MasterCard and neither will you!

Garage Sales and Taxes

In the United States of America, there are two things are certain, death and taxes. If you have the occasional garage sale, taxes will not be an issue. If you are having garage sales every month and making significant income, you will have to file those earnings on your income tax statement. Like Forrest Gump that is all the time when to say about that.

Thanks for reading ***The Ultimate Garage Sale!*** If you have any questions you can reach me at:

glendon@urbanpackrat.com

Check out my blog!

www.urbanpackrat.com for great stories about storage auctions finds and people.

My other books, which can be bought on Amazon.com

Passionate Friday Vol I

Making Money A-Z with Self Storage Auction Units- The Black Edition.

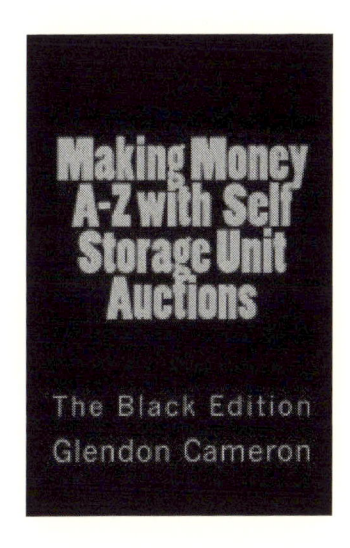

Coming Soon!

What Not To Leave In A Storage Unit! 2010

Stack It Deep Sell It Cheap! How to set up and run a ReSale Store! 2011

"The difference between a successful person and others is not a lack of strength, not a lack of knowledge, but rather a lack of will."

Vince Lombardi

Glendon Cameron is entrepreneur with over eight years in the storage unit auction business. He has bought well over 1250 storage units at auction. In 2002 he got started part time and built it into a 10,000 square foot thrift store. Selling everything from appliances to Gucci shoes! He lives in a suburb of Atlanta, Georgia

Alpena Co. Library
211 N. First Ave.
Alpena, MI 49707

Made in the USA
Lexington, KY
05 March 2011